REA's Books Are The Best...
They have rescued lots of grades and more!

(a sample of the <u>hundreds of letters</u> REA receives each year)

" Your books are great! They are very helpful, and have upped my grade in every class. Thank you for such a great product. "

Student, Seattle, WA

" Your book has really helped me sharpen my skills and improve my weak areas. Definitely will buy more. "

Student, Buffalo, NY

" Compared to the other books that my fellow students had, your book was the most useful in helping me get a great score. "

Student, North Hollywood, CA

" I really appreciate the help from your excellent book. Please keep up your great work. "

Student, Albuquerque, NM

" Your book was such a better value and was so much more complete than anything your competition has produced (and I have them all)! "

Teacher, Virginia Beach, VA

(more on next page)

(continued from previous page)

" Your books have saved my GPA, and quite possibly my sanity. My course grade is now an 'A', and I couldn't be happier. "

Student, Winchester, IN

" These books are the best review books on the market. They are fantastic! "

Student, New Orleans, LA

" Your book was responsible for my success on the exam. . . I will look for REA the next time I need help. "

Student, Chesterfield, MO

" I think it is the greatest study guide I have ever used! "

Student, Anchorage, AK

" I encourage others to buy REA because of their superiority. Please continue to produce the best quality books on the market. "

Student, San Jose, CA

" Just a short note to say thanks for the great support your book gave me in helping me pass the test . . . I'm on my way to a B.S. degree because of you ! "

Student, Orlando, FL

Super Review™

All You Need to Know!

JAVA
with CD-ROM

Randall Raus, M.S.
Computer Engineer and Consultant
Seal Beach, CA

Hang T. Lau, Ph.D.
Adjunct Professor of Computer Science
Concordia University, Montreal, Canada

Research & Education Association
61 Ethel Road West
Piscataway, New Jersey 08854

SUPER REVIEW™
OF JAVA with CD-ROM

Printed in the United States of America

Library of Congress Control Number 00-193096

International Standard Book Number 0-87891-380-7

SUPER REVIEW is a trademark of
Research & Education Association, Piscataway, New Jersey 08854

WHAT THIS Super Review WILL DO FOR YOU

This **Super Review** provides all that you need to know to do your homework effectively and succeed on exams and quizzes.

The book focuses on the core aspects of the subject, and helps you to grasp the important elements quickly and easily.

Outstanding **Super Review** features:

- Topics are covered in logical sequence

- Topics are reviewed in a concise and comprehensive manner

- The material is presented in student-friendly language that makes it easy to follow and understand

- Individual topics can be easily located

- Provides excellent preparation for midterms, finals and in-between quizzes

- Sample codes and programs which encompass all areas of Java – from beginner's level to advanced

- Accompanying CD includes the Java Software Development Kit, and the programs in the text to use on your own computer

- Written by professionals and test experts who function as your very own tutors

Dr. Max Fogiel
Program Director

CONTENTS

About the Java CD-ROM

This CD-ROM contains everything you need to write, compile, and run Java programs and applets.

The CD-ROM contains the following folders:

• Java Source Code: This folder contains the source code for the examples used in the Java Super Review. You use this code to see exactly how Java works, and modify it for your own programs. The *.java files are named according to the sections in which they appear. If you adapt these programs in an attempt to compile them, be sure to change their names to the appropriate class name.

• HTML Files: Some programs require an HTML file to initiate them. These files may be found here.

• Compilable Programs: Most of the code in the Java Super Review is contained in inchoate programs that serve as examples of how programming components are created. Some, however, are complete runnable programs. These are contained in this folder. See the book and SDK documentation for instructions on compiling and running programs, and setting the classpath.

• Java SDK: This folder contains both Windows and Linux versions of Sun Microsystem's Java Software Development Kit.

Java source code will be displayed in `courier`.

CHAPTER 1

Introduction

Among computer languages, Java is most closely related to C/C++, upon which it is based. In fact, in many ways Java is a slimmed down, simpler version of C++. For example, in Java there are no pointers, multiple inheritance, or operator overloading. Java also has automatic memory management capability, relieving the programmer from most of the responsibility of allocating and de-allocating blocks of memory.

Java is more straightforward to program than C/C++ because it is not implementation or platform specific. An example of this is its floating-point numbers which, unlike other languages, are not designed for a specific CPU, but instead conform to the IEEE 754-1985 standard. Thus, the number of bits of a single-precision, floating-point number is the same regardless of the system that is being programmed. In general, Java programs are completely portable. This is achieved by the Java compiler outputting a form of intermediate code known as bytecode, with the bytecode later executed by an interpreter, which *is* system specific.

Another way that Java has made an attempt to be more universal than C/C++ and other earlier languages is by supporting the worldwide Unicode standard for the coding of characters. Java characters can be selected from almost any alphabet, such as Arabic, rather than just the Latin alphabet supported by the ASCII standard.

In some important ways, Java has made a complete break from C/C++. It is an object-oriented programming language that completely severs the ties with procedural programming. There are no functions or procedures in Java. This simplifies the task of programmers and software developers by allowing them to concentrate on the programming of objects.

However, in other respects, there is more to learn in Java because it has added advanced features. There are two types of Java programs: *applets*, which require an Internet browser or an applet viewer, and *stand-alone applications*. Also, Java has extensive library classes and built-in networking capability.

In this Super Review, we will cover, as succinctly as possible, the essentials of Java, beginning with the language fundamentals in Chapter 2, and working our way through more advanced concepts such as applets and custom components.

CHAPTER 2

Fundamentals of the Java Language

2.1 Java Tokens

The basic building blocks of the Java language are called *tokens*. It is important that the Java programmer be familiar with the concept of tokens and how tokens are recognized by the compiler.

When a Java program is compiled, the compiler first removes white spaces not internal to character strings, and line terminators (carriage returns and line feeds). Then, the compiler pulls out tokens. There are six kinds of tokens:

1. **Identifiers**: names chosen by the programmer to identify variables, methods, classes, objects, or labels. Identifiers are case-sensitive.

2. **Keywords**: words reserved by Java. Keywords may not be used as identifiers. Keywords always appear in lowercase.

3. **Operators**: symbols used to represent arithmetic and/or logical operations.

4. **Separators**: symbols used by the Java compiler to divide a program into segments. Examples of separators include the comma " , " and curly braces " { " and " } ".

5. **Literals**: data in the form of numbers or character strings that are explicitly entered into the code. Examples of literals include the integer 32, and the character string "Type Password".

6. **Comments**: technically not considered tokens because they are ignored by the compiler.

2.1.1 Identifiers

The first character of an identifier must be a letter. Subsequent characters can be either letters or numerals. The underscore "_" and the dollar sign "$" are considered letters and may begin an identifier, but this practice should be avoided because many identifiers used by Java's libraries start with the underscore or the dollar sign.

Java is case-sensitive. For example, `My_Integer` and `my_integer` would be considered different identifiers.

Note: Because Java uses the Unicode character set, letters can be from other alphabets other than the Latin alphabet.

2.1.2 Keywords

A complete list of Java reserved keywords—broken down into subcategories—is presented in Table 2.1.

A good way to learn a language is by studying its keywords. Nearly all the keywords in Table 2.1 will be covered either in this chapter or in subsequent chapters. The only exceptions will be the ones reserved for future use by Java, although the programmer still should be aware of them in order to avoid using them as identifiers.

Since Java is case-sensitive and because keywords are always in lower-case, an uppercase or mixed-case keyword is interpreted by the compiler as an identifier. For example, the keyword `int` is used for integer variable declarations. However, `Int` and `INT` would still be accepted by the compiler as valid identifiers.

TABLE 2.1
Reserved Keywords

Data Declaration		Modifier & Access	
boolean	float	final	static
byte	int	native	synchronized
char	long	new	threadsafe
double	short	private	transient
		protected	void
Looping		public	
break	for		
continue	while	**Miscellaneous**	
do		false	return
		import	super
Conditional		null	this
case	if	package	true
else	switch		
		Future Keywords	
Exception		cast	operator
catch	throw	const	outer
finally	try	future	rest
		generic	throw
Structure		goto	var
abstract	implements	inner	
class	instanceof		
default	interface		
extends			

2.1.3 Operators

The complete set of Java operators is shown in Table 2.2.

The arithmetic operators are pretty much standard except for the "%", which is the modulus operator. The modulus gives the remainder. For example, the result of 7 % 2 is 1.

TABLE 2.2
Java Operators

Operator	Description
`=, +=, -=, *=, /=, %=`	Arithmetic assignment
`==, !=, <, <=, >, >=`	Equality and inequality
`+, -, ++, --`	Unary
`&, |, ^`	Bitwise AND, OR, and XOR
`<<, >>, >>>`	Bitwise shift
`=<<, =>>, =>>>, &=, |=, ^=`	Bitwise assignment
`~`	Bitwise complement
`&&, ||`	Logical AND and OR
`? :`	Conditional

The Java arithmetic assignment operators `+=`, `-=`, `*=`, `/=`, and `%=` offer an efficient way to use the original value of a variable to produce a new value:

```
a += b; // means a = a + b
a -= b; // means a = a - b
a *= b; // means a = a * b
a /= b; // means a = a / b
a %= b; // means a = a % b
```

The bitwise AND, OR, and XOR also function as logical operators, so they can be used to evaluate complex Boolean expressions. This is useful to know in the case of "^", because it provides a logical XOR.

These operators cause an entire expression to be evaluated, not just that part necessary to determine if a condition is true or false.

The shift operators perform bitwise shifts on integers or integer variables. The right shift operator >> maintains the sign bit while the right fill shift operator >>> fills the leftmost bit with zeros. Shift operators are demonstrated in Table 2.3.

TABLE 2.3
Shift Operation

x	binary	x << 2	x >> 2	x >>> 2
26	00011010	01101000	00000110	00000110
–19	11101101	10110100	11111011	00111011

The -19 in Table 2.3 is the two's complement of +19, which is formed by inverting each bit, then adding 1.

The unary operators ++ and – – cause a variable to be automatically incremented or decremented. If they appear in front of the variable, the increment or decrement will occur before any binary operation is performed; if they appear after the variable, the increment or decrement will occur after the binary operation. For example:

```
int a, b;      // a and b are declared to be of type int
b = 3;         // the integer 3 is assigned to variable b
a = b++ - 2;   // a is now equal to 1, b is equal to 4
a = ++b - 2;   // b is incremented before the subtraction
               // so b is 5 and a is equal to 3
```

Precedence rules for unary and binary operators will be described in greater detail in Section 2.3.

2.1.4 Separators

Separators are used

1. during the coding phase, to provide the programmer with visual and logical locators,

2. at compile-time, to allow the compiler to divide the code into logical segments, and

3. when the program is executing, to force operator precedence within expressions.

There are six types of separators:

1. ( ) Parentheses are used to open and close a parameter list (particularly when a method is called or declared), or to establish precedence in an expression.

2. [] Brackets are used to open and close an expression that represents the index of an array.

3. { } Curly braces are used to begin and end a block of statements, and also to begin and end an initialization list.

4. ; Semicolons are used as delimiters to mark the end of statements, or as multi-statement blocks, such as in `for` statements.

5. , Commas are used in many contexts to separate the parts of a list.

6. . Periods are used to separate an identifier hierarchy, such as to separate a class name from a method name and are also used as decimal points.

2.1.5 Literals

There are five types of literals: integer, floating-point, boolean, character, and string. A literal may be used to represent a value that is directly assigned to a variable, or as an explicit value that is part of an expression, or as a way to explicitly represent data in an output statement.

Integer Literals

Integer literals can be represented in three number bases in Java: decimal, octal, and hexadecimal. They can also be represented in two sizes: 32-bit and 64-bit. The `long`, or 64-bit, integer literals are designated as such by an uppercase or lowercase "L" at the end. Table 2.4 shows how both 32-bit and 64-bit integers are represented in all three number bases.

TABLE 2.4
Examples of Integer Literals

Integer	Description
348	32-bit decimal integer
9892L	64-bit decimal integer
0X7BC	32-bit hexadecimal integer
0X3FC4L	64-bit hexadecimal integer
04726723	32-bit octal integer
0724L	64-bit octal integer

Floating-Point Literals

The compiler recognizes floating-point literals by the presence of a decimal point, an uppercase or lowercase "E" indicating an exponent, or a float-type suffix. A floating-point literal is not required to have an exponent, a decimal point, or a float-type suffix, but at least one must be included.

The optional float-type suffix is used to indicate the floating-point type. Java has two floating-point types: `float` and `double`. A float is indicated by an uppercase or lowercase "F" at the end (the float-type suffix). A `double` is indicated by an uppercase or lowercase "D". The default is `double`, which is allocated 64 bits of internal storage. A `float` is allocated 32 bits. Table 2.5 shows examples of valid floating-point literals.

TABLE 2.5
Examples of Floating-Point Literals

Floating-Point Literal	Comment
4009.94	Decimal point present
10076e5	Exponent present
2.048E+72	Both exponent and decimal point
.39742e–36	Negative exponent

Boolean Literals

Java takes a simple approach to Boolean literals. Some other languages represent Boolean literals with 0 or 1, or as in the case of C++, false is 0 and any other number is true. In Java, Boolean literals are literally `true` or `false`.

Character Literals

Character literals are always enclosed in single quotes. Some examples are: 'A', 'a', 'x', '4', '+', '?', 'Y', etc. An escape sequence is used to specify nonprintable characters and characters that are part of the escape command itself. Table 2.6 lists the possible escape sequences used to specify character literals.

TABLE 2.6
Character Literals

Sequence	Output	Comment
'a'	a	Any character
'\n'	Linefeed	Line terminator
'\t'	Tab	
'\f '	Formfeed	
'\r'	Carriage return	Line terminator
'\b'	Backspace	
'\"'	Double quote	For string literals
'\''	Single quote	
'\\'	Backslash	Otherwise wouldn't work
'\ddd'	Octal value	Specifies ASCII code
'\xdd'	Hex value	Specifies ASCII code
'\udddd'	Decimal value	Specifies Unicode

The '\udddd' escape sequence, shown in Table 2.6, can be used to specify non-Latin alphabet Unicode characters, as described in the introduction. Also, octal or hexadecimal numbers can be used to directly specify ASCII characters by using the '\ddd' and '\xdd' escape sequences. For example, '\0173' uses octal digits to specify the left curly brace '{' and '\x4B' uses hexadecimal digits to specify uppercase.

String Literals

String literals are enclosed in double quotes. Any characters that are non-printable or that are complicated (such as an internal double quote) can be represented by using one of the escape sequences listed in Table 2.6.

String literals cannot span more than one line; however, the "+" operator can be used to concatenate strings, including strings on more than one line. The compiler does not remove white space from inside double quotes, which is useful when concatenating strings. Some examples of string literals are

"This is a string literal"

"This is an example" + " of concatenation"

"A backslash \\ and double quote \" are done like this"

"The prompt will follow a newline: \n Please Enter Data"

A string literal contains zero or more characters. The null string "" contains zero characters.

2.1.6 Comments

Java has three kinds of comments:

1. the traditional C style

2. the C++ style

3. a slight modification of the C style

The traditional C style begins a comment with a /* and continues for one or more lines until it ends with a */. The C++ style begins with a // and continues only through the end of that line. The following are examples of both:

/* This is the traditional C style of comment which may continue for more than one line */

// This is the C++ style of comment

// which must begin again on each line

Java has added a third style of comment that begins with a /**, continues for one or more lines, and ends with a */. This type of comment is intended for a special documentation program called Javadoc and should be avoided unless used for that purpose.

2.2 Data Types

Variables in Java can be declared as either a *primitive data* type, or as a *reference* type. In this section, we will concentrate on primitive data types. Reference types include arrays, classes, and interfaces. With the exception of arrays, reference types will be left to Chapter 3, Object-Oriented Programming.

There are eight primitive data types in Java. They can be described as follows:

1. byte: 8-bit two's complement integers with values between –128 and +127 (-2^7 to $2^7 - 1$).

2. short: 16-bit two's complement integers with values between –32,768 and +32,767 (-2^{15} to $-2^{15} - 1$).

3. int: 32-bit two's complement integers with values between –2,147,483,648 and 2,147,483,647 (-2^{31} to $2^{31} - 1$).

4. long: 64-bit two's complement integers with values between –9,223,372,036,854,775,808 and 9,223,372,036,854,775,807 (-2^{63} to $2^{63} - 1$).

5. float: 32-bit single-precision floating-point numbers with the smallest being positive or negative 1.40239846e–45 and the largest being positive or negative 3.40282347e+38.

6. double: 64-bit double-precision floating-point numbers with the smallest being positive or negative 4.94065645841246544e–324 and the largest being positive or negative 1.79769313486231570e+308.

7. char: 16-bit characters that conform to the Unicode standard. The smallest numerical value is 0 and the largest is 65,535.

8. boolean: a non-numerical type that has only two values: true or false.

The Java floating-point types conform to the IEEE 754-1985 standard. This means that, in addition to the range of values described above for float and double, there are four additional values defined:

1. zero (0.0e+1)

2. positive infinity (the largest definable positive value plus 1)

3. negative infinity (the largest definable negative value minus 1)

4. non-numeric

2.2.1 Variable Declarations

Variable declaration statements consist of a type name followed by a list of variables, separated by comments, that are declared to be of that type plus any assigned initialization values. In the case of primitive data types, the type name is a reserved keyword. In the case of arrays, the type name may be either a reserved keyword or another identifier assigned to an object. The concept of objects, including arrays of objects, will be discussed in detail in Chapter 3.

The following are examples of variable declarations:

```
byte    byteVar;
short   short_Var, my_Short;
int     int_Var, i = 37, j = 5002;
long    long_Var = 487L;
float   my_Float, X, Y = 3.22e-8f;
double  doubleVar = 4.803e+21;
char    thirdChar = 's';
boolean stillRunning, less_than = true;
```

The default value for all integer and floating-point variables is 0. The default value for an object reference is null. The default value for a boolean is false.

2.2.2 Scope of a Local Variable Identifier

A block is defined as a section of code that begins with a left curly brace "{" and ends with a right curly brace "}". A block-statement consists of zero or more statements surrounded by curly braces. Local variables may be declared anywhere within a block-statement.

A local variable, once declared, is valid within its own block and within any sub-block. However, a local variable declared within a sub-block is only valid within that sub-block. This concept is illustrated below:

```
{
int total, x, y = 3;     //Declare integers
x = 7;
total = x + y;           //total now equal to 10
   {
   int z = 4;            //z declared locally
   total = x + z;        //total, x valid within sub-block.
                         //total = 14

   }
total += z;              //Error! z not valid outside of
                         //its sub-block.

}
```

2.2.3 Arrays

An array is created in two steps:

1. The array is declared with brackets following the array name:

    ```
    int integer_Array [];
    ```

    or the type name:

    ```
    int [] integer_Array;
    ```

2. Memory is allocated for the array by using the keyword new and enclosing the size of the array within brackets:

    ```
    integer_Array = new int [4];
    ```

For arrays with primitive component types, memory can be allocated (without using new), and the array initialized by enclosing the component's values within curly braces:

```
int integer_Array [] = {17, 48, -3, 0};
```

Note: The size of the previous array is 4, because its *initialization list* consists of 4 values.

The range of an index, `i`, of an array whose size is equal to `N` is

```
0 <= i <= (N - 1),
```

In the previous example, `integer_Array []` would have valid index values from 0 to 3, but `integer_Array [4] = 17` would be an error.

Java provides for arrays of arrays. For example:

```
float multi_Array [] [];
multi_Array = new float [3] [4];
```

Arrays of arrays can be initialized as part of a *creation statement* by nesting initialization lists. For example:

```
int multi_Array [] [] = { {3, 28}, {52, 7} };
```

2.3 Evaluating Expressions

Java expressions are evaluated according to three rules:

1. Binary operators are left associative (i.e., if there is more than one operator with the same precedence, the leftmost operator is evaluated first).

2. Unary operators are right associative.

3. Parentheses force operator precedence.

These rules are illustrated below:

```
int a = 2, b = 6, c = 20;   // Initialize a, b, c
int d = -3, e = 2;          // Initialize d and e
int f;                      // Declare f
f = -a + b * (c + d) / e;   // Rule 3 - add c to d first
                            // Rule 1 - multiply by b next
                            // Rule 1 - now divide by e
                            // Rules 1 & 2 - finally add
                            // negative value of a
```

The result of evaluating the above expression would be 49, which would then be assigned to f.

A complete list of operator precedence is presented in Table 2.7

TABLE 2.7
JAVA Operator Precedence

Operator	Description
( ), [ ]	High precedence
+, -, !, ~, ++, --	Unary
*, /, %	Multiplicative
+, -	Additive
<<, >>, >>>	Shift
<, <=, >, >=	Inequality
= =, !=	Equality
&	AND – Bitwise
^	XOR – Bitwise
|	OR – Bitwise
&&	AND – Logical
? :	Conditional
=, +=, -=, *=, /=, %= >>=, >>>=, <<=, &=	Assignment

Boolean Expressions

Boolean expressions are evaluated according to the same rules except the result of each evaluation is always `true` or `false`. The conditional operator ?: (see Table 2.2) takes the following form:

```
boolean-expr ? expression1 : expression2
```

In the above example, `boolean-expr` is evaluated and, if it is `true`, `expression1` is evaluated and that is the value of the conditional; or, if it is `false`, `expression2` is evaluated and that is the value of the conditional. For example:

```
int x = 5, y = 1;
intChar = (3 > x) ? (3 * x) : (4 + x); // intChar = 9
```

2.3.1 Type Conversion

There are two types of type conversion: implicit and explicit. Implicit conversion occurs when an expression includes more than one type. The following rules apply for implicit type conversion:

1. If the increment or decrement operators, ++ and −− , occur as part of an expression, and if the operand is a `byte` or a `short`, it is converted to an `int` and the expression is evaluated. If the operand of the ++ or −− operator is a `long` or a floating-point, it is not converted.

2. If the operands of a binary operator are one of the integer types and one of the operands is a `long`, they are both converted to `long` and the result is a `long`. If neither of the operands is a `long`, they are both converted to type `int` and the result is an `int`, unless it is too large (more than 32 bits), in which case the result is a `long`.

3. If one of the operands of a binary operator is a `float`, then both are converted to `float` and the result is a `float`, unless one is a `double`, in which case they are both converted to `double`.

Java is a *strong type checking* language, so implicit type checking only works without generating a compile error if there is no loss of precision.

Explicit type conversion involves *casting*, which is illustrated below:

```
int round, I = 5;
float x = 222.7f, y = 4.83F;
round = ( (int) (x / y)) + I; // Result of x/y cast as int
```

The casting of an expression to a new type can be done by prefixing the expression with the new type name in parentheses. Any of the four integer types can be cast as any of the other four integer types, although there may be a loss of data. Also, the char type can be cast as an integer type.

2.4 Control Structures

Java's control structures are similar to control structures in other languages.

2.4.1 Conditional Statements

The if statement has the following general form:

```
if (boolean-expression) statement;
else statement;
```

or

```
if (boolean-expression)
{
   statement(s);
}
else
{
   statement(s);
}
```

The else portion of an if statement is optional.

A variation of the if statement is the switch statement, which has the following general form:

```
switch (expression)
{
```

```
case value:
   statement(s);
      break;
case value:
   statement(s);
      break;
default:
   statement(s);
      break;
```

The *expression* above must evaluate to a char, a byte, a short, or an int. The keyword break is optional, but program control will fall through to the next statement if it is not present. The default is also optional.

The following illustrates the use of the if and switch statements:

```
int intVar, i = 4, j = 5;  // Initialize variables
char charVar = 0;          // CharVar now is null
if ( ( (i - 4) == 0) && ( (j - 3) != 0) )
{
   charVar = 'B';
}
switch (charVar)            // Single character expression
{
   case 'A':
      intVar = 1;
      break;
   case 'B':
      intVar = 2;          // Should execute this
      break;
   default:
      intVar = 3;
      break;

}
```

2.4.2 Looping Statements

The while loop has the following general form:

```
while (boolean-expression)
```

```
{
    statement(s);
}
```

The do-while loop, designed to guarantee at least one execution of the loop body, has the general form:

```
do
{
    statement(s);
}
while (boolean-expression)
```

The for loop has the following general form:

```
for (initialization; test condition; modification)
{
    statement(s)
}
```

If a while, do-while, or for loop has a loop body of only one statement, the curly braces are optional.

break and continue Constructs

In a loop, if a break statement is encountered, the loop is exited immediately. If a continue statement is encountered, program control will return to the beginning of the loop without executing the remainder of the loop body.

If one loop is nested within another, the break_label construct can be used to break out of the inner loop. In this case, program control is transferred to the end of the loop that is labeled. A compile error will be generated if the break_label construct is used with a nesting level of more than two.

The looping statements along with the break and continue constructs are illustrated by the following code:

```
class SimpleClass {
    public static void main (String [] args)
    {
        int outer = 0;
```

```java
int int_Array []; // while loop will initialize array
int_Array = new int [10];
OuterLoop:          // label for outer loop
while (outer < 10)
{
  for (int ctr = 0; ctr < 10; ctr++)
  {
    int_Array [ctr] += ctr;
    if ( (ctr % 3) > 3)
      continue;
            // skip rest of inner loop
    int_Array [ctr] = 3 * ctr;
    if ( (ctr % 3) > 4)
      break OuterLoop; // break out of inner loop
  }
  if (int_Array [outer] > 50)
    break;
                    // break out of while loop
  outer += 1;
  System.out.println (outer);
  }
  System.out.println (outer);
  }
}
```

The first break statement, break OuterLoop, will cause program control to go to the end of the while loop because it is the loop labeled OuterLoop:. The second break statement will cause program control to break out of the while loop.

2.5   A Simple Application Program

Below is an example of a simple application program. It should be saved in a file with the same name as the primary class (the class that contains the main() method). The file extension for Java source code files is .java on Windows systems and on UNIX systems.

```
// Hello.java
//
import java.io.*;
public class Hello {
  public static void main (String [] args) {
    System.out.println ("HELLO WORLD!");
  }
}
```

The Java Development Kit (JDK) version 1.3 can be downloaded from Sun Microsystems Web site at http://java.sun.com. The unpacking program will automatically install JDK. Before compiling, it is necessary to add the c:\jdk1.3\bin path and the c:\jdk1.3\lib\jar.tools path to the environment variable of the autoexec.bat file. The bin directory contains the compiler and the interpreter, and the jar.tools file contains the class libraries.

The above program can be compiled by the following command:

```
javac Hello.java
```

The Java interpreter can then be called to execute the program `Hello` by the following:

```
java Hello
```

The output should be:

```
Hello World!
```

Every Java application program must contain a `main()` method, which is where execution is initiated. The `System.out.println()` method is supplied by the Java class library and directs output to the standard output device. The `main()` method and the `System.out.println()` method will be discussed in greater detail in subsequent chapters.

The other kind of Java program is the *applet*. Applets were designed to be run on the Web, and will be the subject of Chapter 6.

CHAPTER 3

Object-Oriented Programming

Programs written in procedural programming languages are organized into callable subprograms such as procedures and functions. Unfortunately, the data worked on internally by a subprogram only "lives" while the subprogram is being executed. This ultimately results in the main program keeping track of the data that is outside the scope of the subprograms. Since the main program maintains much of the data, it is impossible to effectively test and debug programs in smaller, more manageable modules. Thus, much of the testing and debugging has to be done on the entire program, which can be a complicated, difficult, and time-consuming process.

Java programs are entirely made up of logical units called *objects*. In contrast to procedures and functions, an object's data is maintained as long as that object is needed. This allows the programmer to encapsulate all of the data and methods needed for a particular task into an object, a separate logical unit. Because an object has its own data and methods, once it has been thoroughly tested, it can be thought of almost as a black box—as long as it works, the programmer does not have to worry about what is inside.

Since the main method of a Java application program is required to maintain only a very small amount of data (the objects keep track of most of the data), it is possible to test and debug programs in separate modules. Thus, the strictly object-oriented approach of Java sharply reduces the time spent debugging.

Object-oriented languages have additional advantages. A feature called *inheritance* allows the programmer to build a hierarchy of structures, with more and more complex objects being created as extensions of simpler ones. Another feature called *polymorphism* allows dissimilar objects to be utilized by their common attributes.

3.1 Classes

A class is a set of data (variables global to the class, called *fields*) and the methods needed to manipulate that data. A class definition has four parts:

1. the class declaration (`class NewClass`)

2. the opening curly brace "{"

3. the class body: the field declarations and method definitions

4. the closing curly brace "}"

For example:

```
class NewClass {
   . . .
   class body
   . . .
}
```

A class is a template for an object, although that object will not exist until a program statement creating an *instance* of that class is executed. The following is an example of code statements that will create an instance of the class `NewClass`:

```
NewClass NC;
NC = new NewClass ();
```

The first statement declares `NC` to be an object of the type `NewClass`. Next, the second statement allocates the memory space and machine code necessary for an instance of `NewClass` to exist. The set of parentheses following `NewClass` would normally contain the parameter list (variables and literals, separated by commas, used to initialize the object). If there is no parameter list, parentheses are still required. In any case, once the two statements have completed, messages may be sent to, and operations carried out by, the object NC.

The following is an example of a class (with a defined body):

```
class Square {
  int number;
  int computeSq () {
    return (number * number);
  }
}
```

The variable number above, is an example of a field declaration, and computeSq() is an example of a method definition. The *members* of a class are its fields and methods. The method computeSq() has a return type of int. It is a simple method with no parameters, but if computeSq() did define a parameter list, it would have been within the parentheses. The body of computeSq() is a single line that returns the square of number.

The class Square is instantiated and has an operation carried out on it by the following code:

```
int x;
Square Sq = new Square (); // Create instance of Square
Sq.number = 2;             // Send object Sq a message
x = Sq.computeSq ();       // Carry out operation, x = 4
```

In the second line above, an object of the class Square is created in one statement. This is allowed in Java, although using two statements is often more convenient, as will become clear.

An object is an instance of a class, or an array. The variable created in an object declaration statement represents a reference to an object, not the object itself. For example, the following is legal:

```
NewClass NC1 = new NewClass ();  // Create two
NewClass NC2 = new NewClass ();  // instances of NewClass.
NC2 = NC1;                       // Both now reference
                                 // same instance.
```

3.1.1 Class Declarations

Class declarations take the following form:

```
access-modifier    type-modifier    class    ClassName
extends    SuperClassName    implements    interFaceNames
```

There are two *access-modifiers*: public and the default. Members of a public class (its fields and methods) are accessible by any other class or object including those outside its own *package*. (The Java package, the topic of Section 3.3, is a group of classes that makes up a compilation unit.) If there is no access modifier, the default is a "friendly" class. Members of friendly classes are accessible by any class or object within its own package. It is important to be aware that each class member must also be declared with the appropriate access modifier, if it is to have the desired accessibility. Access modifiers of members is covered in Sections 3.1.2 and 3.2.

There are three *type-modifiers*: abstract, final, and the default. Abstract classes may not contain code that creates new instances, nor is it permissible for other classes to contain code that creates new instances of an abstract class.

Abstract classes may contain abstract methods. Abstract methods define return type, name, and parameters, but no method body. Abstract classes normally are used as *superclasses* which are *extended* by *subclasses*. If a class *extends* a superclass that contains abstract methods, then it must *implement* those methods. An example that illustrates the use of the abstract and extends keywords appears at the end of this section.

Final classes may not be extended. In some cases, a class may fulfill its intended purpose, so the programmer may not want it extended.

Following the keyword class is the class name. If the keyword extends is included in the class declaration, then the class is a subclass whose superclass is identified by *SuperClassName*. Being a subclass means that the class inherits all of the non-private members (fields and methods) of its superclass. The subclass may access inherited members by their simple names, except when an inherited field is *hidden* by a subclass field with the same name, or an inherited method is *overridden* by a subclass method with both the same name and *parameter signature*. In these cases, the superclass members must be accessed by *qualified names*, using the super keyword. Examples of hidden fields, overriding methods, use of the super keyword, and use of qualified names will be presented and discussed in subsequent sections.

If the keyword implements is included in the class declaration, then the class implements one or more *interfaces*. Interfaces will be discussed in Section 3.5.

Below is an example that illustrates the use of the abstract and extends keywords. The abstract class Securities is a generalized class that defines an abstract method, unitPrice(). Securities is extended by the class Stocks, which fully implements unitPrice(). Because Stocks implements all of its superclass's abstract methods, it may be declared without the abstract modifier. However, such a class may still be declared abstract if the programmer does not want the class instantiated.

```
public abstract class Securities {
  protected float totalValue;
     . . .
protected abstract float unitPrice ();
                // Abstract method
}
public class Stocks extends Securities {
  int nbr_of_Shares;
     . . .
  protected float unitPrice () {
                // Fully implemented method
    return (totalValue / nbr_of_Shares);
  }
}
```

3.1.2 Class Variables

There are three kinds of variables declared in a class:

1. **Fields:** variables that are accessible and modifiable by every method in the class. These variables are usually declared immediately

following the class's opening curly brace, although they can be declared anywhere in the class as long as they are not declared within a method.

2. **Method Variables:** variables declared within the body of a method (local variables), or within a method's formal parameter list (their rules differ slightly from local variables). Method variables will be discussed in Section 3.2.

3. **Variables Declared Within Static Initializers:** If a variable is declared using the `static` modifier, it may optionally be initialized by a static initializer—a block-statement that contains executable code. Variables declared within a static initializer are local variables. For example:

```
static long x = {int y = 4; x = 2 * y;};
```

Fields can be further broken down into two kinds of variables:

1. **Static Variables:** variables declared using the `static` modifier. Also called *class variables*, they have the same value for every instance of a class. They can be accessed by qualified names that include either the class name, or the name of an object. For example:

```
NewClass NC1 = new NewClass (); // Create object
NewClass NC2 = new NewClass (); // Create object
NewClass.staticVar = x;  // Only one copy of staticVar,
NC1.staticVar = x;       // so all three statements do
NC2.staticVar = x;       // the same thing.
```

2. **Instance Variables:** variables that are accessed by the same name for every instance of the class, but are allocated separate memory locations—allowing them to have different values for each object. They cannot, however, be accessed by their class name. Instance variables are also known as *instance fields*. For example:

```
NewClass obj1 = new NewClass (); // Create object 1
NewClass obj2 = new NewClass (); // Create object 2
obj1.nonStaticVar = 2;   // Two copies of nonStaticVar
obj2.nonStaticVar = 9;   // exist, and they contain
                         // different values: 2 and 9.
```

The following are modifiers that can be used for declarations of field variables:

1. **public:** Fields accessible to all classes including those outside the current package.

2. **protected:** Fields accessible to all classes within their own package.

3. **private:** Only the methods within the current class may access private fields.

4. **default:** If there is no access modifier, the default is that field variables are accessible within their own class, and by any class within the current package. However, subclasses outside the current package cannot access these fields.

5. **static:** Fields whose values are the same for all instances of the class (as discussed earlier).

6. **final:** A final field's value may not change during program execution. A final field will have the same values for all instances, and if it is also declared static, it will only require one memory location.

In the following example, the generalized class Securities is extended by a more specific class Bonds.

```java
public abstract class Securities {
  protected float totalValue;
  protected static int current_Date [];
     . . .
  protected abstract float unitPrice ();
                         // Abstract method
}
public class Bonds extends Securities {
  static final String investment_Type = "bonds";
  String issuer;          // Name of Govt. agency or
                          // Corp. that issued bond.
  int date_of_Issuance [], date_of_Maturity [];
  private float interest_Rate;
     . . .
  protected float unitPrice () {
                          // Fully implemented method
    return (totalValue / nbr_of_Bonds); }
  float annualIncome () { // To be developed further
```

```
    return (interest_Rate * totalValue); }

}
```

In the previous example, `current_Date` and `investment_Type` were declared to be `static` fields because they apply to all instances of their respective classes.

With the use of the `final` modifier for the declaration of `investment_Type`, the programmer can be assured that its value won't be inadvertently changed during program execution. The modifier `protected` makes `current_Date` accessible from anywhere in its own package, and from outside its own package, in the case of a `Securities` subclass.

Special Variables `this` and `super`

Java has special variables that are represented by the keywords `this` and `super`. The special variable `this` is used to explicitly reference the current object, and the special variable `super` is used to explicitly reference a method of the superclass.

If a subclass and a superclass declare fields with the same name, the superclass field is hidden in the subclass. (Note: This holds true even if the type and the modifiers of the subclass field are different from the hidden superclass field.) However, the superclass field can still be accessed using the `super` keyword. For example, a hidden superclass field `doubleVar` could be assigned the value of the subclass field by the following:

```
super.doubleVar = doubleVar;
```

The `this` special variable is often used to access a field that is hidden by a local variable, which will be shown in the next section. But the important thing to remember about `this` is that it refers to "this" object—meaning the current object. Consider the following use of `this`:

```
class Point {
  int x, y;
  NewPoint NP;
  void findNewPt () {
    NP = new NewPoint ();
    NP.setNew_w (this);
```

```
    NP.setNew_z (this);
  }
}
class NewPoint {
  int w, z;
  void setNew_w (Point pt) { w = pt.x + 1; }
  void setNew_z (Point pt) { z = pt.y + 1; }
}
```

The findNewPt() method above supplies this as the parameter when it invokes the methods NP.setNew_w() and NP.setNew_z(). Since this represents the current object, and since the code where it appears is in a Point class, it is most likely that the current object is a Point object. An examination of the parameter declaration of setNew_w shows that it is indeed a Point object. This is also true for setNew_z.

There are some cases, however, when the current object is not an instance of the enclosing class. For example, when a static method is executed, the object that invoked the static method is the current object.

3.2 Methods

Methods, in Java, are similar to C/C++ functions. A method definition consists of four parts:

1. the method declaration

2. the opening curly brace {

3. the method body

4. the closing curly brace }

A method declaration takes the following form where everything in italics is optional:

```
access-modifier method-modifier return-type
Method_Name (parameter-list) throws exception(s)
```

Since both methods and fields are members of their class, or interface, the same *access-modifiers* apply. These include: public, private, protected, and the default.

There are five *method-modifiers*:

1. **static:** No other method with the same name may be defined in the same class or subclass. Static methods operate only on `static` variables.

2. **final:** It is possible to define a method with the same name in the same class or subclass, but they must have different *signatures*, i.e., different number and/or type of parameters.

3. **abstract:** Methods that have a declaration part, but have no method body. Abstract methods are implemented (and fully defined with a method body) in a subclass of the `abstract` class.

4. **synchronized:** Used as a safeguard to ensure that a method is accessed in the correct sequence when multiple threads of a program are simultaneously executed (covered in Chapter 4).

5. **native:** Indicates that a method will be written in a native language such as C/C++.

Methods may return a value, in a way similar to functions in procedural languages. The method return-type may be any valid Java data type including object types, or if the method does not return any value, the return type is declared `void`.

The *parameter-list* of a method includes zero or more parameters, and can be shown by the following:

```
modifiers return-type Method_Name (Type param1,
Type param2, ...)
```

Variables declared within the body of a method are local variables. Other local variables include variables declared within the header of a `for` loop, or within static initializers. Local variables declarations are similar to declarations of field variables, with the exception that local variables declarations do not have modifiers. Local variables do not have to be declared until they are needed, and their scope is from the declaration statement to the end of the current block, or sub-block. Local variables hide field variables by the same name, but the `this` keyword can be used to access the field (as will be shown in the next example).

Variables declared within the parameter list of a method are not local variables. They are different in the sense that only one variable of each type is declared, and they are initialized by the parameters that are passed to the method. However, their scope is the body of the method, and they are still considered method variables.

Exceptions will be discussed in Chapter 4—Exception Handling, I/O Streams, and Threads.

3.2.1 Overloading and Overriding of Methods

Methods may be *overloaded* by other methods with the same name and return type, as long as they are in the same class or a subclass of the original method. However, the method signature, the name of the method, and the number and type of the parameters, must be different. If two methods have different return types, or have different parameter names, the method signature still may be the same. For example:

```
public String get_Sec_Type (boolean prn_out) {
  if (prn_out)
    return ("Investment type = " + investment_Type);
  else return investment_Type;
}
byte get_Sec_Type (boolean get_sub) {
    if (get_sub) return subId;
    else return id;
}
```

The above methods have the same signature because they have the same name, get_Sec_Type, and the same number and type of parameters—exactly one parameter of type boolean. The above code would result in a compile error if they appeared in the same class.

Methods may be *overridden* by methods in the subclass of the original method's class. In order for a method to override a method of the superclass, the method signature must be the same. If a method overrides another method, it must not have a greater degree of access protection. In other words, a protected method cannot override a public method.

The super keyword allows the programmer to override a method without completely rewriting it. For example, the Securities superclass might have an annualIncome() method that computed capital gains. In this situation, the subclass Stocks could override this method to compute the dividend of the income, but still rely on the superclass method of the same name to compute the capital gains. This could be done using the super keyword, as illustrated below:

```
protected float annualIncome (float prevTotal) {
    float capGains = super.annualIncome (prevTotal);
    return (capGains + (dividend * Nbr_of_Shares));
}
```

3.2.2 Constructors

A *constructor*, if it exists, is a method with the same name as its class. It is called automatically when an instance of that class is created. Constructors perform certain tasks, such as the initialization of variables, that are needed to set up an instance of a class. Since constructors do not return a value, they are either declared with the void return type or no return type. It is allowable to overload constructors as long as the parameter signature is different. This allows the programmer the flexibility to create instances of the same class in different ways. It is also possible for a constructor method to invoke the constructor of its super class using the super keyword.

The following example shows how class constructors work:

```
public abstract class Securities {
    protected float totalValue;
    protected static int current_Date [];
        . . .
    public Securities (float amount, int current_Date []) {
        this.current_Date = new int [3]; // Create array
        setDate (this.current_Date, current_Date);
        totalValue = amount;
    }

        /* setDate() is a generalized method for setting the
           date. */
    public void setDate (int date_1 [], int date_2 []) {
        for (int i = 0; i < 3; i++) date_1 [i] = date_2 [i]; }
}
public class Stocks extends Securities {
```

```
static final String investment_Type = "stocks";
String issuer;          // Name of Company that issued
                        // stock.
final byte subId = 2;   // subId: 1 = preferred, 2 = common
private byte id;        // id: 1 = NYSE, 2 = NASDAQ
...
```

```
// Constructor for subclass Stocks follows.
  public Stocks ( String corp, byte id,
    float amount, int date [] ) {
```

```
// Next statement calls constructor in superclass
    super (amount, date);
    issuer = corp;       // Name of Corp. that issued
                         // stock.
    this.id = id;        // this means this object.
  }
}
```

3.2.3 Polymorphism

Polymorphism is a capability that allows an object of a given class to assume multiple forms, either as an object of one of its subclasses, or of its own class. For example, objects of the Stocks or Bonds classes are also objects of the Securities class. The method shown below would work fine if it were handed a Bonds object, or a Stocks object, even though the first parameter is declared to accept a Securities object.

```
float get_Income (Securities sec, float prevTotal) {
  return sec.annualIncome (prevTotal); }
```

For example:

```
float prev = 1855.23f, stockIncome;
Stocks stks;
stockIncome = get_Income (stks, prev); // Works fine
```

Actually the preceding example is somewhat limited since only the subclasses may be instantiated. This is because their superclass, Securities, is abstract. However, in cases where the superclass is not abstract, both superclass and subclass objects may be used polymorphically.

3.3 The Java Package

Packages provide a way to organize code by placing similar classes and/or interfaces (interfaces are discussed in Section 3.5) into one package. Also, packages allow the programmer to hide classes that are intended only for internal use by an application. Finally, packages provide a way to handle the layers of access security that were described earlier in this chapter for classes, variables, and methods.

A package statement is used to declare a file's classes to be part of a package. A package statement must be the first statement in a file, and takes the form:

package *packageName;*

For example:

package funds;

Hierarchies of package structures can also be created. If, for example, the package funds was declared with two subpackages, pension and insurance, the package statements for files in the two subpackages would be

package funds.pension;
package funds.insurance;

All of the files that are declared to be in the same package should be stored in the same directory. The Java compiler creates a separate file for each class, then either stores them in the same directory as the source file, or the directory specified by an optional command line directive. The compiler converts the package statements to directory pathnames, which at runtime, are used by the interpreter to locate compiled class files. This means that the directory structure must reflect the package hierarchy. If a call to a method took the following form:

funds.pension.investments.Bonds.unitPrice();

then, on a Windows system, the underlying directory and file structure would be:

\funds\pension\investments\Bonds.class

and the CLASSPATH statement in the autoexec.bat file would have set the CLASSPATH so that its last directory was immediately above the funds directory:

```
set CLASSPATH=C:\ROOT_DIR\FUNDS_PARENT_DIR
```

The code for the method unitPrice() would be located in the file Bonds.class. Since the Bonds class is public, the compiler would have created it from a file named Bonds.java (a source file may have only one public class). The Bonds.java file would be in a directory named investments, and the first noncomment line in the investments file would be the package statement:

package funds.pension.investments;

To add to the readability of long pathnames, it is conventional to capitalize the first letter of class names. Also, it is conventional to capitalize one or more letters, but not the first letter of a method name, if it is likely to be accessed outside its own package (see above example of Bonds class).

3.3.1 Import Statements

If a number of classes are in the same directory, but not part of a package, they can be used by other classes. However, they must be imported first. For example:

import Securities;

If the same classes are included as part of a package, they can be used by any class in that package without importing them or without including the package name as part of a pathname.

If a class is outside the current package, it can be used in three ways:

1. By prepending the package name to the class name. For example, an instance of the class stocks would be declared as follows:

    ```
    funds.pension.investments.Stocks stock_Obj;
    ```

2. By importing the entire package first. For example:

```
import funds.pension.*;
Stocks stock_Obj;
```

3. By importing the individual class. For example:

```
import funds.pension.investments.Stocks;
Stocks stock_Obj;
```

Import statements can be anywhere in the code as long as they appear before the class to be referenced. If an entire package is imported, more RAM is required and the program may be less efficient, so it is desirable to import classes individually, if only a few classes are needed.

3.4 Example of an Application Program

The program that follows is the result of combining most of the methods and fields from this chapter's previous examples. This includes nearly all of the members that appeared in examples involving the `Securities`, `Stocks`, and `Bonds` classes. Some minor differences include dropping the `get_Sec_Type()` methods that illustrate method overloading. These have been replaced by the non-overloaded `get_Stock_Id()` and `get_Bond_Id()`. Another minor difference is that the `annualIncome()` method of the `Bonds` class has had a line added, allowing it to invoke its overridden counterpart.

The directory structure required for this example to run on a Windows system is as follows:

classpath_dir\funds\pension\investments

where *classpath_dir* is the directory specified by the `set CLASSPATH` command, either in the autoexec.bat file, or on the command line.

There is only one file in the pension directory, Securities.java. This file contains the `Securities` class, and is part of the `funds.pension` package. `Securities` was included in this package to show that `protected` members can be accessed from within subclasses. The other files are part of the `funds.pension.investment` package, and consist of Stocks.java, Bonds.java, and Manage.java. The Manage.java includes the primary class (the one with the `main()` method) and a non-public class (a file may have only one public class).

None of this application's files are in the funds directory, but funds must be included in the package name, or the Java interpreter will not find the files. This is because the JDK (Java Development Kit) hierarchy begins just below the *classpath_dir* directory. In other words, funds is just below the directory specified by the CLASSPATH, so it begins with a valid package name.

The Data class, which hasn't appeared before, contains the data needed to initialize both Stocks and Bonds objects. Data also includes methods to invoke the constructors of the Stocks and Bonds classes.

Notice that the main() method appears to be creating objects without the new keyword. Actually, the Data class methods initShares() and initBonds() return Stocks and Bonds objects, which are created using the new keyword.

All the fields of the primary class Manage are declared static. The reason for this is that they are accessed by a static method, the main() method. In many applications, the main() method instantiates the primary class to avoid the necessity of declaring static fields. This technique will be illustrated in future examples.

This program (and its directory structure) can be found on the CD. To execute, type the following commands:

```
javac Manage.java
java funds.pension.investments.Manage
```

The compiler will use the package names and import statements to find the other source files: Bonds.java, Stocks.java, and Securities.java. If a .class file already exists and the .java source file is more recent, then javac will recompile the source file.

```
// Securities.java

package funds.pension;

public abstract class Securities {
  protected float totalValue;
  protected static int current_Date [];

  public Securities (float amount, int current_Date [])
  {
```

```java
      this.current_Date = new int [3]; // create array
      setDate (this.current_Date, current_Date);
      totalValue = amount;
   }
//setDate() is a generalized method for setting the date

   public void setDate (int date_1 [], int date_2 []) {
      for (int i = 0; i < 3; i++) date_1 [i] = date_2 [i]; }

   protected abstract float unitPrice (); // abstract method

   protected float annualIncome (float prevTotal) {
      return (totalValue - prevTotal); } // capital gains
}
//
// Stocks.java
//

package funds.pension.investments;
import funds.pension.Securities;

public class Stocks extends Securities {
   int nbr_of_Shares;
   static final String investment_Type = "stocks";
   String issuer;          // Name of company that issued
                           // stock.
   final byte subId = 2; // 1 = preferred, 2 = common
   private byte id;        // 1 = NYSE, 2 = NASDAQ
   private float dividend;

   // constructor for subclass Stocks follows.

   public Stocks ( String corp,  byte id,
                   float amount, int date [] ) {

   // next statement calls constructor in superclass
      super (amount, date);

      issuer = corp;  // Name of corp that issued stock.
      this.id = id;   // this means this object
```

```
}

void setDividend (float annual_Div) {
  // accessor method for annual dividend.
  dividend = annual_Div;
}

protected float unitPrice () {
  // fully implemented method
  return (totalValue / nbr_of_Shares);
}

protected float annualIncome (float prevTotal) {
  float capGains = super.annualIncome (prevTotal);
  return (capGains + (dividend * totalValue));
}

byte get_Stock_Id (boolean get_id) {
  if (get_id) return id;
  else return subId;
  }
}


//
// Bonds.java
//
package funds.pension.investments;
import funds.pension.Securities;

public class Bonds extends Securities {
  int nbr_of_Bonds;
  static final String investment_Type = "bonds";
  String issuer;          // Name of corp. that issued bond.
  final byte subId = 2; // 1 = foreign, 2 = domestic
  private byte id;        // id: 1 = U.S Treasury
                          // 2 = Corp,
                          // 3 = Municipal

  int date_of_Issuance [], date_of_Maturity [];
  private float interest_Rate;
```

```java
    // constructor for subclass Bonds follows.

    public Bonds  ( String agency,  int date_C [],
                     byte id,         int date_M [],
                     float amount,   int date_I [] ) {

       // next statement calls constructor in superclass
       super (amount, date_C);

       issuer = agency;  // agency that issued bonds
       this.id = id;     // this means this object

       /* create arrays, then invoke super class method to
          set dates */

       date_of_Maturity  = new int [3];
       date_of_Issuance  = new int [3];
       setDate (date_of_Issuance, date_I);
       setDate (date_of_Maturity , date_M);
   }

void setRate (float rate) {
   // Accessor method for interest rate
   interest_Rate = rate;
}

protected float unitPrice () {
   // fully implemented method
   return (totalValue / nbr_of_Bonds);
}

protected float annualIncome (float prevTotal) {
   float capGains = super.annualIncome (prevTotal);
   return (capGains + (interest_Rate * totalValue));
}

byte get_Bond_Id (boolean get_id) {
   if (get_id) return id;
   else return subId;
   }
}
```

```java
//
// Manage.java
//
package funds.pension.investments;

public class Manage {
  static float annualDiv = .03f;
  static float interest_Rate = .07f;
  static boolean id = true, sub = false;
  static float spr = 122936.50f, bpr = 91723.00f;

  public static void main (String args []) {
    System.out.println ("Here");
    Data dt = new Data ();

    Stocks stk = dt.initShares ();
    stk.setDividend (annualDiv);

    System.out.print (
      '\n' + "Type = " + stk.investment_Type +
      '\n' + "Company = " + stk.issuer +
      '\n' + "Share price = " + stk.unitPrice () +
      '\n' + "Annual Income = " + stk.annualIncome (spr) +
      '\n' + "Stock Id = " + stk.get_Stock_Id (id)  +
      '\n' + "Stock sub Id = " + stk.get_Stock_Id (sub) +
      '\n' );

    Bonds bnd = dt.initBonds ();
    bnd.setRate (interest_Rate);

    System.out.print (
      '\n' + "Type = " + bnd.investment_Type +
      '\n' + "Agency = " + bnd.issuer +
      '\n' + "Bond price = " + bnd.unitPrice () +
      '\n' + "Annual Income = " + bnd.annualIncome (bpr) +
      '\n' + "Bond Id = " + bnd.get_Bond_Id (id) +
      '\n' + "Bond sub Id = " + bnd.get_Bond_Id (sub) +
      '\n' );
  }
}
```

```
class Data {
    int date_C [] = { 3, 23, 2001 };   // today's date
    int date_M [] = { 8, 11, 2013 };   // 30 year bonds
    int date_I [] = { 8, 11, 1983 };   // date of issuance
    float totalStockValue = 147870.00f;
    int nbrShrs = 2790;
    float totalBondValue = 99000.00f;
    int nbrBnds = 90;
    byte stock_Id = 1;   // NYSE (New York Stock Exchange)
    byte bond_Id = 1;    // U.S. Treasury Bonds
    String corp = "ATT";
    String agency = "Treasury Dept.";
    Stocks stks;
    Bonds bnds;

    Stocks initShares () {
        stks = new Stocks (corp, stock_Id,
                            totalStockValue, date_C);
        stks.nbr_of_Shares = nbrShrs;
        return stks;
}

Bonds initBonds () {
    bnds = new Bonds (agency, date_C,
                      bond_Id, date_M,
                      totalBondValue, date_I);
    bnds.nbr_of_Bonds = nbrBnds;
    return bnds;
    }
}
```

If the above program was executed, the output would be the following:

```
Type = stocks
Company = ATT
Share price = 53.0
Annual Income = 29369.6
Stock Id = 1
Stock sub Id = 2
Type = bonds
```

```
Agency = Treasury Dept.
Bond price = 1100.0
Annual Income = 14207.0
Bond Id = 1
Bond sub Id = 2
```

Note that the interest_Rate field in the Bonds class and the dividend field in the Stocks class are encapsulated by declaring them private. These private fields are set by what are called "accessor" methods: setDividend() and setRate() (which are non-private). It is recommended that accessor methods begin with either "get" or "set". An overriding method must have the same level of protection as the method it overrides. For example, the unitPrice() methods in both the Bonds and Securities classes have the protected level of access.

3.5 Interfaces

Although Java does not allow multiple inheritance (a subclass may not have more than one parent class), it does allow a class to implement more than one interface.

An interface defines the broad general outlines of how a class might be implemented by defining constants and abstract methods, then leaves the details to the class that implements it. The following is an example of an interface:

```java
public interface Memory {
   static final byteLength = 8;
   static final wordLength = 4;
   int computeBits (int nbr_Words);
}
public class Computer implements Memory {
   int computeBits (int nbr_Words) {
     return (nbr_Words * byteLength * wordLength)
   }
}
```

It is common practice for an application to implement interfaces that are included in packages supplied by the Java library.

3.6 Nested Classes

Nested classes and interfaces are defined as members of *enclosing* classes, or as *local* classes, within a block of code. There are two types of nested classes:

1. **Static Nested Classes:** explicitly declared static. These may not access the non-static members of their enclosing class. Nested interfaces are implicitly static, although they may be declared static explicitly.

2. **Inner Classes:** non-static nested classes. An inner class may be defined as a top-level *member* class, or as a named or *anonymous* *local* class.

3.6.1 Static Nested Classes and Interfaces

Static nested classes and interfaces are defined within another class for the sake of convenience. They are members of the enclosing class, and as such, have the same accessibility options as other class members. For example, suppose a class was defined for the purpose of modeling hotels in a convention-oriented beach city:

```
package conventions;
public class Hotels { // Enclosing class for PowerStatus
    int roomsReserved, roomsEmpty;
    float occupancy;
    static boolean elevator, power, lobby, finished =
                                        true;
    static String hotel_1 = "Sand'n'Surf", hotel_2 =
                                        "Breakers";
    static String lastChecked;
    ...
public static PowerStatus {        // Static nested class
    boolean running = true, on = true, open = true;
    public boolean morningShift () {
        lastChecked = hotel_1;
        elevator = running;
        power = on;
        lobby = open;
```

```
    return finished;
    }
  }
    // Rest of Hotel class methods goes here
}
```

Assuming methods and fields of `PowerStatus` may be useful to other classes, it would helpful if it was made `public`. Since its enclosing class is `public`, `PowerStatus` has the option of public accessibility. If `PowerStatus` were to be used by a class in the same package, its qualified name would be `Hotel.PowerStatus`, and the qualified name for the `morningShift()` method would be `Hotel.PowerStatus.morningShift()`. If `PowerStatus` were used by a class in a different package, its qualified name would be `convention.Hotel.PowerStatus`. If a class in the same package wanted to access the `morningShift()` method by its simple name, it could do the following:

```
import Hotel.PowerShift;
done = morningShift ();
```

A possible limitation of the `PowerStatus` nested class is that several fields of `Hotel` (e.g., `boolean elevator`) were declared static to provide direct accessibility to the methods of `PowerStatus`. If `Hotel` was instantiated, it might become necessary to create multiple copies of these static fields. The next section shows how this limitation is overcome by non-static nested classes (inner classes), which are capable of being instantiated within an object of the enclosing class. But first, here are a few final words on static nested classes. Static nested classes may be nested to any depth, although good programming practice usually uses a depth of less than two or three. Finally, a static nested class may not be defined within an inner class.

3.6.2 Inner Classes

Inner classes are used when the methods of a nested class must access the instance fields, including the private instance fields, of the enclosing class. Theoretically, the functions performed by the inner class could be implemented by adding code to the enclosing class. Often, however, it is desirable to restart an operation, or create more than one object associated with the enclosing object. This kind of situation is much more compatible with instantiable objects, especially if access is required to the private members of another object.

There are other advantages to using inner classes, one of which is the "helper" code appearing adjacent to the appropiate enclosing class members in the program listing. Another advantage is that it is often more convenient to implement an interface using an inner class, because the inner class can consist almost entirely of the implemented interface methods. In other words, the implementation of the interface is all in one place, avoiding confusion.

The following class was designed to manage investment funds (continuing with our `Securities` class examples). The `FundManager` class contains two inner classes that provide the function of helper classes. The first inner class, `Fund`, provides the members necessary to create a linked list of investments (stocks and bonds) that represent a fund. The second inner class, `LinkableInvestment`, is nested inside the first inner class.

The `import` statements at the beginning of the package do not include imports from `funds.insurance`, or `funds.annuity`. The reason for this is to avoid the minor modifications of the `Securities`, `Stocks`, and `Bonds` classes that would justify putting them into another directory. The code of this class assumes that there are three types of funds being managed, not just one. Aside from the import statements, the most confusing line of the `FundManager` program is:

```
node.setNext ( node.getNext().getNext() );
```

The above statement, from the `Remove()` method, removes a linked security node from a fund. It uses a reference, `node`, to access a method, `getNext()`, which returns a `LinkableSecurity` reference, `next`, which accesses the method, `getNext()`, to return another `LinkableSecurity` reference. The last reference is stored in `node`, allowing a node to be removed.

When tracing through the following class, it should be remembered that there is an interface at the end, `LinkableSecurity`, that is referenced in the `FundManager` class. Just as easily this interface could have been moved to provide an example of a static nested interface.

```java
package funds;
import funds.pension.Securities;
import funds.pension.investments.Stocks;
import funds.pension.investments.Bonds;


class FundManager {

  Fund funds [];   /* A Fund is a linked list of investments.
                      funds[] is an array of linked lists. */

  static final String pensionFund = "pension",
                      annuityFund = "annuity",
                      insuranceFund = "insurance";

  final byte maxNbrFunds = 10;    // Max. # of funds managed
  private byte curNbrFunds = 0; // Current number of funds

// Constructor for FundManager class

  FundManager () { funds = new Fund [maxNbrFunds]; }

  byte setUpFund (String fund_Type, String fund_Owner)
  {
// The current number of funds must be less than the maximum.

    if (curNbrFunds >= maxNbrFunds) return -1;

// The fund type must match at least one valid fund type.

    else if  ( (fund_Type != pensionFund) &&
               (fund_Type != annuityFund) &&
               (fund_Type != insuranceFund) ) return -1;

// A similar fund must not already exist.

    for (byte i = 0; i < curNbrFunds; i++)
      if ((funds [i].organization == fund_Owner) &&
          (funds [i].type_of_Fund == fund_Type)) return -1;
```

```
// Set up new fund and return fund index.

    funds [curNbrFunds] = new Fund (fund_Type, fund_Owner);
    return curNbrFunds++;
  }
  public void purchase (byte fund_index, Securities bought)
    { funds [fund_index].add (bought); }
  public void sale (byte fund_index, Securities inv_sold)
    { funds [fund_index].remove (inv_sold); }

/* private */ class Fund {
  String type_of_Fund, organization;
  LinkableSecurity head = null;
  Securities lastTransaction;/* Last purchase or sale of
                              security (stock or bond) */

// Constructor for Fund class

  Fund (String type, String org) {
    type_of_Fund = type;
    organization = org;  /* union, insurance co., city
                            govt., etc., that owns fund */
  }
  void add (Securities purchased) {
    lastTransaction = purchased;
    head = new LinkableInvestment ();
  }
  void remove (Securities sold) {
    LinkableSecurity node = head;
    if ( sold == head.getInv() ) head = head.getNext();
    else while (node != null) {
      if ( sold == node.getNext().getInv() ) {
          node.setNext ( node.getNext().getNext() );
          return;
      }
      node = node.getNext();
    }
  }
}
private class LinkableInvestment implements LinkableSecurity {
```

```
LinkableSecurity next;
Securities investment;

// Constructor for LinkableInvestment class

  LinkableInvestment () {

/* The last transaction must have been a purchase, or
the constructor for this class would not have been
invoked.*/

  investment = lastTransaction;
  next = head; /* When returns, head will equal this
               instance of LinkableInvestment. */
}
public Securities getInv () { return investment; }
public LinkableSecurity getNext () { return next; };
public void setNext (LinkableSecurity node) {next=node;};

} // End of LinkableInvestment inner class
} // End of Fund inner class
} // End of FundManager top-level class

interface LinkableSecurity {
  Securities getInv ();
  LinkableSecurity getNext ();
  void setNext (LinkableSecurity node);
}
```

An important characteristic of inner classes is that they are members of the enclosing class like any other member. Inner classes can be assigned any access modifier that would work with any other member of the class. For example, the above Fund and LinkableInvestment inner classes are both defined to be private member classes, allowing a high degree of protection.

Because member classes can be nested to any level, a new form of this, new, super syntax was required to implement member classes. For example, if A, B, and C were nested classes, with class C enclosed in class B, and class B enclosed in class A, a field in class A can be referred to explicitly by:

```
A.this.fieldOfA;
```

The same concept holds true for the use of the new and super keywords. In general, the syntax is the name of the class containing the member being referred to, a dot, then the keyword, then another dot, then the name of the member. For example:

```
objName = A.new ClassName ();
A.super.methodOfA();
```

3.6.3 Local Classes

Local classes may only be defined as part of an executable block-statement (usually within the body of a method, but also within a static initializer). Local classes have access to any variable within its scope that is declared final, including method parameters.

The concept of an access modifier is meaningless at the local level, so local classes may not be declared public, protected, or private. Also, a local class may not be defined with the static keyword.

Local classes have access to the members of the enclosing class. This requires the use of a new syntax for the keyword this (same syntax as the one used by member classes). The keywords new and super are not used in local classes.

Local classes are often used to implement event listeners for graphical user interfaces. An example of an event listener implementation will be presented in Section 7.2.2.

Anonymous Classes

Anonymous classes are local classes that are defined without a name. They are used in much the same way as local classes with names. An example will be shown in Section 7.2.2.

CHAPTER 4

Exception Handling, I/O
Streams, and Threads

4.1 Exception Handling

The term *exception* in Java is used in two contexts:

1. to refer to an error condition that halts the flow of execution, and

2. to an object that contains information about the error.

Classes whose instances contain information about an exception are either subclasses of the Error class or subclasses of the Exception class. Both the Error class and the Exception class reside in the `java.lang` package.

The information contained in `error` objects is used by Java to handle nonrecoverable errors—usually resulting in program termination. The information contained in `exception` objects can be used by the user program to handle recoverable errors.

The Exception subclasses reside in five packages: `java.awt`, `java.io`, `java.lang`, `java.net`, or `java.util`. In order for a program to handle a particular exception, the appropriate Exception subclass, or the package containing the appropriate Exception subclass, must be imported. A list of some commonly thrown exceptions is presented in Table 4.1.

TABLE 4.1
Commonly Thrown Exceptions

ArithmeticException	IndexOutOfBoundsException
ArrayIndexOutOfBoundsException	InterruptedException
ClassNOtFoundException	InterruptedIOException
EOFException	MalFormedURLException
FileNotFoundException	SocketException
IOException	UnknownHostException

Exception objects (instances of the classes in the above table) are created to allow the exception *handler* to identify the type of exception. Once the exception handler identifies the type of exception, it takes the appropriate action. There are two types of exception handlers: (1) throws clauses, discussed in the next section, and (2) try statements. The general form of a try statement is shown below:

```
try {
   statement(s);
}
catch (ExceptionType1 ExceptionObj) {
   statement(s);
}
catch (ExceptionType2 ExceptionObj) {
   statement(s);
)
   ...
finally {
   statement(s);
}
```

As can be seen from the previous example, a try statement is similar in structure to a switch statement. If there is at least one catch method, the finally method is optional; otherwise, it is required. If the body of a try, catch, or finally method consists of only one statement, curly braces are not required.

If one of the statements following the try keyword throws an exception, the Java interpreter skips the rest of the try block, looks for a catch construct whose parameter list matches the thrown exception, then executes the first matching catch method. The remainder of the catch methods are skipped. If a finally method has been defined, it is always executed.

An example of a try statement will be presented in Section 4.1.2. However, in order to provide some insight into when exception handlers are required, user-defined exceptions will be discussed in the next section.

4.1.1 User-Defined Exceptions

User-defined exceptions may be defined by extending the Exception class of the java.lang package, for example:

```
class NbrOutOfRangeException extends Exception {
  NbrOutOfRangeException () {
    super ();      // Constructor for super class
  }
  NbrOutOfRangeException (String msg) {
    super (msg); // Constructor for super class
  }
}
```

The above code uses the declaration part to define the name of the exception, specifically NbrOutOfRangeException. The class body consists of two constructors that call the constructor of the superclass – the Exception class. The Exception class has two constructors. The first returns an object which identifies the exception only by class name. The second returns an object that contains additional information about the exception in a string message. In theory, a user-defined exception class can be further customized by adding fields and additional methods, but this is seldom needed.

`throw` and `throws` Keywords

The `throw` keyword can be used to throw a user-defined exception. The `throws` clause must be present in a method declaration if (1) a method has the potential to throw a user-defined (or a Java-defined) exception, and (2) the method does not contain a `try` statement to handle the user-defined exception, as shown below:

```
class NbrOutOfRangeException extends Exception {
    // Code to implement exception goes here
}
class ProcessArray {
    // Array declaration goes here
  int doubleInt (int intNbr)
        throws NbrOutOfRangeException {
    if (intNbr > 50) {
      NbrOutOfRangeException e =
        new NbrOutOfRangeException ("Too Large");
      throw e; // Throw exception object
    }
    else if (intNbr < 10) {
      NbrOutOfRangeException e =
        new NbrOutOfRangeException ("Too Small");
      throw e; // Throw exception object
    }
    return (intNbr * 2);
  }
// Array processing method goes here
}
```

In the above example, since the `throws` clause is used, the calling method must have an exception handler, either a `try` statement, or a `throws` clause, which would throw the exception further up the Java hierarchy.

4.1.2 Handling a Thrown Exception

Many of Java's operations can result in a potentially recoverable exception being thrown. The exceptions classes listed in Table 4.1 are defined by Java to allow a program to identify and attempt to recover from exceptions caused by Java-defined operations. Also, user-defined exception classes can be created to identify exceptions thrown by user-defined methods.

Some operations which are part of Java's library classes include code in their method definitions to throw an exception. For example, the declaration for the `FileInputStream` constructor is

```
public FileInputStream (String filename)
throws FileNotFoundException {
```

If a Java operation contains code to throw an exception in its method definition, a compile-time error will be generated unless an appropriate exception handler—a `throws` clause or a `try` statement—is included in the calling method. The compiler does not require an exception handler for some exceptions, such as the `ArrayIndexOutOfBoundsException`. To find out which exceptions require exception handling, the programmer can consult Java's online documentation, or a Java class library reference book, or simply rely upon compile-time error messages.

An example of a `try` statement that handles a thrown exception is presented below:

```
class NbrOutOfRangeException extends Exception {
  NbrOutOfRangeException () {
    super ();      // Constructor for super class
  }
  NbrOutOfRangeException (String msg) {
    super (msg);  // Constructor for super class
  }
}
class ProcessArray {
  int intArray [] = {5, 23, 19, 37, 59};

  int doubleInt (int intNbr)
          throws NbrOutOfRangeException {

    if (intNbr > 50) {
      NbrOutOfRangeException e =
        new NbrOutOfRangeException ("Too Large");
      throw e;  // Throw exception object
    }
    else if (intNbr < 10) {
```

```
            NbrOutOfRangeException e =
                new NbrOutOfRangeException ("Too Small");
            throw e;  // Throw exception object
        }
        return (intNbr * 2);
    }
    void doubleArray () {
        short nbrFinally = 0;
        for (int i = 0; i <= 5; i++) {
            try {
    // Next line may throw 2 possible exceptions
                intArray [i] = doubleInt (intArray [i]);
            }
            catch (NbrOutOfRangeException e) {
                if (e.toString () == "Too Large")
                    intArray [i] = 0;
                else if (e.toString () == "Too Small")
                    intArray [i] = -1;
                System.out.println (e.toString () +
                            ", Array Index = " + i);
            }
    // Next line catches exception if i >= 5
            catch (ArrayIndexOutOfBoundsException e) {
                System.out.println (e.toString () +
                            ", Array Index = " + i);
        }
    // Finally, keep track of number of times
    // finally block is executed.
            finally { nbrFinally += 1; }
        }
        System.out.println ("Executed finally clause " +
            nbrFinally + " times");
    }
}
public class TestProcessArray {
    public static void main (String args []) {
        ProcessArray process = new ProcessArray ();
        process.doubleArray ();
    }
}
```

The previous example includes a try, catch, and finally statement. The try method contains a block of code that can throw two possible exceptions. The first is a user-defined exception, NbrOutOfRangeException, that can potentially be thrown by the doubleInt method. If NbrOutOfRangeException is thrown, it is caught by the first catch method which then checks if the integer was too large or too small before taking the appropriate action. The second possible exception, ArrayIndexOutOfBoundsException, is a Java-defined exception, which would be thrown on the last iteration of the for loop, because the IntArray index would be out of bounds when i = 5. This exception would be caught by the second catch method, allowing the program to recover. Note: The second catch method has no body, but one is not required. The finally method is used to keep track of the number of exceptions.

4.2 Input/Output Streams

A *stream* is a sequence of data blocks sent one at a time from a producer process to a consumer process. The data blocks could be anything, from a byte, to a primitive data type, to a complex object. The data that leaves the producer process is called an *output stream*, and the data that arrives at the consumer process is called an *input stream*.

Streams are unidirectional. A consumer cannot use an input stream to send information back to a producer. Although some of the methods of input stream classes allow the consumer some flexibility, such as backing up to an earlier point, this capability is actually provided by Java's internals. However, a consumer can create an output stream back to the producer, thus, still achieving two-way communication.

A stream can be considered an input stream from the standard input device (usually the keyboard) or an input stream from a file, or a stream can be an output stream to the standard output device (usually the display) or an output stream to a file. The subject of streams is very complex and could be the subject of another book in itself. This section will concentrate on the more basic streams. Streams will also be discussed further in Section 5.3.

4.2.1 Input/Output (Byte) Streams

All Java classes are derived from the Object class which resides in the `java.lang` package. The classes that provide the functionality used to input and output a stream of bytes form two three-stage-hierarchies, and although descended from the Object class, they reside in the `java.io` package.

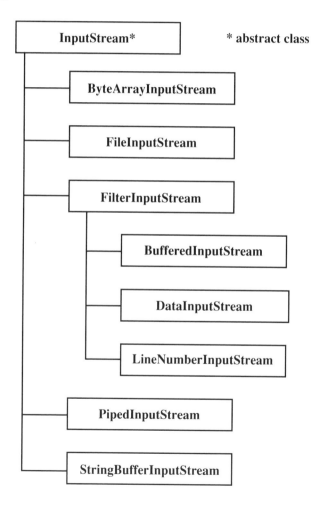

Figure 4.1 Input Stream Classes

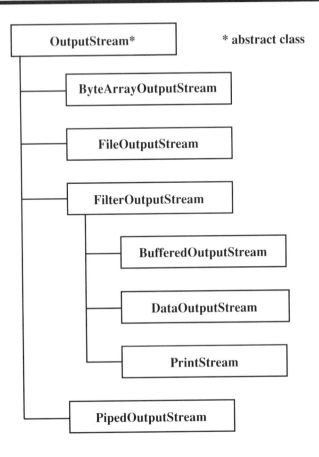

Figure 4.2 Output Stream Classes

Figure 4.1 shows the input stream class hierarchy and Figure 4.2 shows the output stream class hierarchy. InputStream and OutputStream are abstract classes which define the basic methods inherited by all input and output streams. These methods are presented in Tables 4.2 and 4.3 respectively.

TABLE 4.2
Public Methods of InputStream Class

Method	Description
int read (*byte*[] buffer, *int* offset, *int* count)	Reads number of bytes in count, beginning at offset, into buffer. Returns number of bytes read, or -1 if end-of-file.
int read (*byte*[] buffer, *int* count)	Returns number of bytes read, or -1 if end-of-file.
long skip (*long* count)	Skips the number of bytes contained in count from this input stream. Returns number actually skipped.
int available()	Returns the number of bytes that can be read from input stream without blocking.
void mark (*int* limit)	Marks the current position in the input stream so that a later call to reset() will reposition it. limit is the maximum number of bytes to allow to pass before resetting.
boolean markSupported()	Returns the availability of mark-reset support for stream.
void reset()	Resets to position previously marked.
void close ()	Closes input stream. Actually meant to be overridden by subclasses of InputStream.

TABLE 4.3
Public Methods of OutputStream Class

Method	Description
void write (*byte*[] buffer, *int* offset *int* count	Writes number of bytes in count, from buffer beginning at offset.
void write (byte[] buffer)	Writes all members of byte array buffer.
void flush()	Flushes any buffered bytes from this output stream.
void close()	Closes the output stream.

All reads are based on a blocking read. When a read method is called, it will not return until all of the data requested has been read or an exception occurs. The available() method can be used to determine how many bytes can be read without blocking. All writes are based on a blocking write. When a write method is called, it will not return until all the data to be written has been accepted or an exception occurs.

4.2.2 Second Level of Input and Output (Byte) Stream Hierarchy

The second level of the input and output (byte) stream hierarchy consists of more specialized classes (see Figures 4.1 & 4.2). Instances of these classes are used for the following purposes:

1. ByteArrayOutputStream and ByteArrayInputStream— to provide byte streams to and from byte arrays

2. PipedOutputStream and PipedInputStream—to provide byte streams to and from concurrently executing threads

3. FileOutputStream and FileInputStream—to provide byte streams to and from files

4. `ObjectOutputStream` and `ObjectInputStream`—to provide serialization and deserialization of objects (including arrays and strings) and primitive data (`int` fields, `float` fields, etc.).

Note: Serialization is the process of converting an object, or a primitive data value, to a sequence of bytes (a stream), and deserialization is the same process in reverse.

`PipedInputStream` and `PipedOutputStream` Classes

Data can be sent through a `PipedOutputStream` by one concurrently executing thread and received through a `PipedInputStream` by another thread. Although these represent two classes, they can be conceptually thought of as one pipe. In effect, the `PipedOutputStream` pipe fits into the `PipedInputStream` pipe, creating a single data pipe. The declaration of a pipe stream is shown below:

```
PipedOutputStream pipeOut = new
     PipedOutputStream ();
PipedInputStream pipeIn =
     new PipedInputStream (pipeOut);
```

The pipe objects, once created, can be passed as parameters to the two parallel threads, or if one of the two communicating threads creates the pipe, it can hand the other thread either the input or the output pipe. We will show examples of pipe streams as we cover more advanced applications. Figure 4.3 depicts the flow of data between threads.

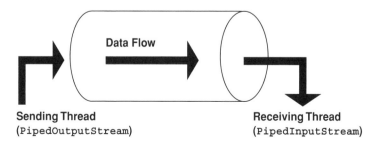

Sending Thread
(`PipedOutputStream`)

Receiving Thread
(`PipedInputStream`)

Figure 4.3 Pipe Stream

`FileInputStream` and `FileOutputStream` Classes

Objects of the `FileInputStream` and `FileOutputStream` classes provide basic file reading and writing capabilities.

The `FileInputStream` class has three constructors, whose declaration parts look like this:

```
public FileInputStream (String FileName) throws
    FileNotFoundException
public FileInputStream (File FileObj) throws
    FileNotFoundException
public FileInputStream (FileDescriptor FileDescriptorObj)
```

The argument of the second constructor is an instance of the File class. The File class will be described in more detail in Section 4.2.5. The argument of the third constructor is a `FileDescriptor` object. A file descriptor is a compact representation of the information needed to manipulate an open file or device. File descriptors are seldom needed to write to and read from files.

The `FileOutputStream` class has three constructors:

```
public FileOutputStream (String FileName) throws
    IOException
public FileOutputStream (File FileObj) throws
    IOException
public FileOutputStream (FileDescriptor FileDescriptorObj)
```

The `FileOutputStream` constructors are the close counterpart of the `FileInputStream` class except that the first two potentially throw a different exception (`IOException` rather than `FileNotFound`).

4.2.3 (Byte) Stream Hierarchy Filter Streams – Third Level of Input and Output

Subclasses of `FilterInputStream` and `FilterOutputStream` (see Figures 4.1 & 4.2) provide streams that result in the input or output being filtered in various ways:

1. `BufferedInputStream` and `BufferedOutputStream` provide buffered input and output that is more efficient,

2. DataInputStream and DataOutputStream provide for deserialization and serialization of primitive data types,

3. PushbackInputStream allows parsing of the input, and

4. PrintStream is used to output the Unicode representation of Java primitive data types and objects.

DataInputStream and DataOutputStream Classes

Data read through a DataInputStream is filtered in such a way that it can be interpreted as primitive data types. The following are the DataInputStream methods that allow primitive data types to be read:

```
readBoolean()        readByte()        readChar()
readDouble()         readFloat()       readInt()
readLong()           readShort()       readUnsignedByte()
readUnsignedShort()
```

The declaration part for the DataInputStream constructor is the following:

public DataInputStream (InputStream InputStreamObj)

A good example is constructing a DataInputStream with an instance of the FileInputStream class as the InputStream parameter. Then primitive data types could be read from a file.

Data written through a DataOutputStream is filtered in such a way that it can be interpreted as primitive data types. The following are the DataOutputStream methods that allow primitive data types to be written:

```
writeBoolean()       writeByte()       writeChar()
writeDouble()        writeFloat()      writeInt()
writeLong()          writeShort()
```

The declaration part for the DataOutputStream constructor is:

public DataOutputStream (Outputstream OutputStreamObj)

4.2.4 Standard Input/Output Device Streams

The abstract System class, which cannot be instantiated or extended, is responsible for runtime related functions and the security manager.

The System class also provides objects, so they do not have to be created, for streams to and from the standard input and output devices (usually the keyboard and the display, respectively). The object used for input from the keyboard is System.in, and the object used for output to the screen is System.out. System.in is an instance of the InputStream class and System.out is an instance of the PrintStream class. The next example shows a method that outputs a prompt to the display, then reads in a file name from the keyboard. Note the use of "+" as a separator in the code below:

```java
import java.io.*;
class FileReadWrite {
      . . .
  String getFileName () {
    byte buffer [] = new byte [80];
    final int maxNmLn = 8, exLn = 3;
    try {
      System.out.print ( 'n' + 'n' +
        "File name length = " + maxNmLn + 'n' +
        "Extension length = " + exLn + 'n' +
        "Please enter file name: ");
      System.in.read (buffer);
    }
    catch (IOException e) { System.exit (1); }
    return (new String (buffer, 0));
      . . .
  }
}
```

In the above example, the System.out.print () is an overloaded method of the class PrintStream. Depending on its parameter signature, print () will serially output the Unicode representation of a primitive data type, a primitive data type literal, a string, a string literal, or any combination thereof. There is also the alternative System.out.println() method, which is the same as print () except that it adds a line terminator. The read () of System.in.read () is an overloaded method of the InputStream class (see Table 4.2).

On the third line of the `try` block in the previous example, a constructor of the String class is used to convert the ASCII values of the `byte` stream that was read into buffer to its Unicode equivalent.

4.2.5 Working with Files and Streams To and From Files

The File class does not have stream capability, but it is still an important part of the `java.io` package. `File` can be used to create a file or directory. The `FileInputStream` and `FileOutputStream` classes are provided for creating files, but they do not have the equivalent methods of the File class for working with files. Some of these methods are listed below. In nearly all cases, their function is obvious by the method name. For example, `length()` returns the length of the file.

```
getName()          getPath()          isHidden()
isDirectory()      isFile()           length()
lastModified()     setReadOnly()      canWrite()
canRead()          delete()           exists()
```

The three forms of the `File` constructor are shown below:

```
public File (String filename)
public File (String parentname, String childname)
public File (File parentname, String childname)
```

When an instance of `FileInputStream` is created, a file is opened and an input stream from that file is made available. The read methods inherited from InputStream can be used to input a sequence of bytes. When the program is finished reading the file, the `close()` method is used, as shown in the segment below:

```
import java.io.*;

class FileReadWrite {

  String getFileName () {
    // body of getFileName()
  }

  void readFromFile (String fileName) {
    int count = 1024, offset = 0, nbrBytesRd = 0;
    byte buffer [] = new byte [count];
```

```
  try {
    FileInputStream infile;
    infile = new FileInputStream (fileName);
      // On next line read method return the
      // number of bytes actually read
    nbrBytesRd = infile.read (buffer, offset, count);
    infile.close ();
  }
  catch (FileNotFoundException e)
    { System.out.print ("File not found " + '\n'); }
catch (IOException e) {
    System.out.print ("I/O error" + '\n');
    System.exit (2);
}

// Print out contents of file

for (int i = 0; i < nbrBytesRd; i++)
  System.out.println ( " Byte [" + i +
      "] = " + buffer [i] );
}

  // remaining members of class FileReadWrite
}
```

The constructor of the `FileOutputStream` class can be used to create a new file, and since it inherits the methods of OutputStream, `write()` can be used to write data to the file (see the `writeToFile()` method below). The following example shows the complete `FileReadWrite` class, including the `getFileName()` and `readFromFile()` methods previously discussed. Also shown is the `TestFileReadWrite` class whose `main()` method drives the members of `FileReadWrite`.

```
import java.io.*;
class FileReadWrite {
  String getFileName () {
    byte buffer [] = new byte [80];
    final int maxNmLn = 8, exLn = 3;
    try {
      System.out.print ( '\n' + '\n' +
```

```
        "File name length = " + maxNmLn + '\n' +
        "Extension length = " + exLn + '\n' +
        "Please enter file name: ");
      System.in.read (buffer);
    }
    catch (IOException e) { System.exit (1); }
    return (new String (buffer, 0));
  }
  void readFromFile (String fileName) {
    int count = 1024, offset = 0, nbrBytesRd = 0;
    byte buffer [] = new byte [count];
    try {
      FileInputStream infile;
      infile = new FileInputStream (fileName);
        /* On next line read method return the
           number of bytes actually read. */
      nbrBytesRd = infile.read (buffer, offset, count);
      infile.close ();
    }
    catch (FileNotFoundException e)
      { System.out.print ("File not found " + '\n'); }
    catch (IOException e) {
      System.out.print ("I/O error" + '\n');
      System.exit (2);
    }

    // Print out contents of file

    for (int i = 0; i < nbrBytesRd; i++)
      System.out.println ("Byte [" + i + "] = " + buffer
                                  [i]);
  }
  void writeToFile (String fileName) {
    int count = 5, offset = 0;
    int iA [] = { 12, 98, 104, 39, 42 };
    byte buffer [] = new byte [count];

// Cannot initialize byte array, must cast from int array.
    for (int i = 0; i <= 4; i++) buffer [i] = (byte) iA [i];
    try {
      FileOutputStream fs;
```

```
            // Each of next three lines potentially
            // throws an IOException
          fs = new FileOutputStream (fileName);
          fs.write (buffer, offset, count); // Returns void
          fs.close ();
        }
      catch (IOException e) {
          System.out.print (e.toString () + "I/O error");
          System.exit (3);
        }
      }
    }
public class TestFileReadWrite {
    public static void main (String args []) {
      String fileNm;

      // Create file read/write object

      FileReadWrite frw = new FileReadWrite ();

      fileNm = frw.getFileName (); // Get file name
      frw.writeToFile (fileNm);     // Write to file
      frw.readFromFile (fileNm);    // Read from file
    }
}
```

4.2.6 Reader and Writer (char) Streams

The reader and writer char streams are analogous to the input and output byte streams, with the difference that they are intended to handle text applications. The char stream/byte stream counterparts are as follows:

1. The abstract Reader and Writer classes are the counterparts of the abstract InputStream and OutputStream classes.

2. FilterReader and FilterWriter are the counterparts of FilterInputStream and FilterOutputStream.

3. BufferedReader and BufferedWriter are the counterparts of BufferedInputStream and BufferedOutputStream.

4. `CharArrayReader` and `CharArrayWriter` are the counterparts of `ByteArrayInputStream` and `ByteArrayOutputStream`.

5. `PrintWriter` is the counterpart of `PrintStream`. The structure of the `Reader` and `Writer` (char) stream classes is shown in Sample Program 4.4.

4.3 Threads

A *thread* is a light-weight version of a process. Multiprocessing using the traditional fork command involves creating an exact duplicate of the variables and machine code of the original process. For this reason, multiprocessing in languages such as C/C++ involves considerable overhead. Also, because a process once created is completely independent, interprocess communication tends to be difficult.

Java allows the programmer to spin off a thread that uses only the variables and code needed for concurrent execution, making threads much less expensive. Communication between threads is simpler than interprocess communication because multiple threads can access each other's data. The tradeoff Java makes for ease of communication and less overhead is an increased risk of multiple threads interfering with each other's data.

A threadable class (capable of parallel execution) must either implement the `Runnable` interface or extend the Thread class. Both the `Runnable` interface and the Thread class are found in the `java.lang` package. A class that implements `Runnable` must define the interface's `run()` method. A class that extends `Thread` must override the `run()` method of its superclass.

Although a class that implements `Runnable` will usually include fields and methods other than the `run()` method, a simple implementation of `Runnable` is shown below:

```
class Parallel implements Runnable {
  public void run () {
    // code to be executed in parallel ...
  }
}
```

The Parallel class may be spun off as a separate thread by following these three steps:

1. Declare a variable p to be the reference to an object of the Parallel class, and create an instance of Parallel with the new operator. Java allows both of these operations to be combined in one statement.

2. Create an instance of the Thread class, pThread—passing the runnable object, p, to the class's constructor.

3. Invoke the start() method of the Thread class, as shown below:

```
Parallel p = new Parallel ();      // Step 1.
Thread pThread = new Thread (p);   // Step 2.
pThread.start ();                  // Step 3.
```

The second way of making a class runnable as a thread is by extending the Thread class and overriding its run() method. A simple example of an extension of Thread is shown below:

```
class ParallelThread extends Thread {
  public void run () {
    // code to be executed in parallel ...
  }
}
```

The ParallelThread class may be spun off as a separate thread by following these two steps:

1. Create an instance of ParallelThread (the Thread subclass).

2. Invoke the start() method of the Thread class, as shown below:

```
ParallelThread pThread = new ParallelThread (); // Step 1.
pThread.start ();                                // Step 2.
```

The above techniques may seem straightforward, but unfortunately, the implementation of threads is one of the most complicated and confusing aspects of Java. There are several reasons for this:

1. Threads need to communicate. The most convenient way to accomplish this is to have the parent (the class that creates an instance of the threadable class) pass a reference of itself to the thread's constructor. This allows the thread to access the parent's data and methods. An example will be presented later in this section.

2. Other techniques are used to communicate between threads. Pipe streams are commonly utilized for inter-thread communication.

3. The `java.applet.Applet` and the `java.lang.Thread` classes both include methods named `start()`, `stop()`, and `destroy()`. Since applets often spin off threads, and both classes have methods with similar names, it can sometimes be confusing whether an Applet method or a Thread method is being invoked. Also, the `Applet stop()` and the `Thread stop()` methods do not perform corresponding functions for their respective classes—the `Applet stop()` method temporarily suspends an applet, while the `Thread stop()` method effectively destroys a thread. In fact, the `Thread stop()` method does almost the same thing as the `Thread destroy()` method. The programmer must remember to use the `Thread suspend()` method if execution is to be resumed. The `Thread resume()` method can then be used to resume the thread's execution.

4. Consider the main thread of execution. Both applet programs and application programs have a primary class. The primary class of an applet is the one which contains the `init()` method. The primary class of an application program is the class which contains the `main()` method. The main thread of execution of an applet begins with the `init()` method, and the main thread of execution of an application begins with `main()` method. The main thread of execution continues as other methods of the primary class are invoked, or methods of other classes are invoked by the primary class. Often, the main thread will spin off other threads—but the main thread will continue to execute in parallel. However, if the primary class does not extend `Thread`, or does not implement `Runnable`, it won't have access to most Thread methods. An exception to this is that it can invoke the

`Thread.sleep()` method because it is defined as a static method.

5. A class that extends the Thread class has direct access to the methods of the Thread class, while a class that implements the `Runnable` interface does not. The programmer must be careful to use only qualified names (e.g., `pThread.sleep()`) when accessing Thread methods—if the thread was created from a class that implements `Runnable`.

6. Often Java programmers create threads in different ways. For example, the constructor of a threadable class is sometimes used to not only create an instance of a thread, but also to start it running. It is good programming practice to allow the constructor to return, then complete the steps necessary to initiate parallel execution. As we discussed earlier, for classes that implement the runnable interface, there are three steps necessary to create and start a thread. It is clearer for these three steps to appear as three consecutive statements. Also, for classes that extend the Thread class, there are two steps necessary to create and start a thread—ideally these steps should appear in consecutive statements. Comparisons of these kinds of programming practices will be included in an example in this section.

4.3.1 An Example of the Use of Threads by an Application

While applets are run by applet viewers or browsers, application programs are run by the Java interpreter. The interpreter begins execution by invoking the `main()` method. All application programs are required to define a `main()` method, and it must be included in a public class—referred to as the primary class. The `main()` method will be discussed in more detail in Chapter 7, but for now, the reader should be aware that `main()` is the interpreter's entry point.

Sample Program 4.4 shows an application program that creates instances of four threadable classes. The functions performed by four of these threadable classes are very simple, and nearly identical—incrementing a counter. However, inter-thread communication is implemented in a variety of ways, to illustrate points made in the previous section. There is also a fifth thread—the main thread. The main thread takes advantage of the fact that `Thread.sleep()` is a static method—to allow more processing time for threads it has spun off.

Sample Program 4.4 Example of Parallel Threads

```java
public class PrimaryClass {

    /*These four variables are declared as references to
    objects that will be used to create four separate
    threads of execution in spinOffThreads()). */

    Parallel_1 p1;              // reference to runnable obj.
    ParallelThread_2 pThread2;  // reference to thread object
    Parallel_3 p3;              // reference to runnable obj.
    ParallelThread_4 pThread4;  // reference to thread object

    /*These two variables are references to thread objects
    that will be used in conjunction with the two runnable
    references (above) to create the first and third
    separate threads of execution in spinOffThread(). */

    Thread pThread1;        // reference to thread object
    Thread pThread3;        // reference to thread object

    boolean keepCounting;   // If true, threads will
                            // increment ctr1 thru ctr4.
    int ctr1 = 0, ctr2 = 0, ctr3 = 0, ctr4 = 0;

    // Constructor for primary class

    public PrimaryClass () {
      keepCounting = true;
    }

    /* This method creates new instances of four threads
       and starts them running.*/

    private void spinOffThreads () {
```

/* The first of the following two statements creates a
   new instance of Parallel_1. Although Parallel_1 does
   not extend Thread (it implements Runnable), a new
   thread is created and started in two steps, instead of
   three, because p1.start() is relied upon to create the
   thread instance. Note: p1.start() is not a Thread
   class method, it is an arbitrarily named method of the
   Parallel_1 class. */

```
p1 = new Parallel_1 (this);
p1.start ();
```

/* The next statement creates a new instance of
   ParallelThread_2, and since ParallelThread_2 extends
   Thread, a new thread is created. A thread is created and
   started from a Thread subclass in one step, instead of
   two, because the constructor of ParallelThread_2 is
   relied upon to start the thread. Note: The current
   object (this) is passed as a parameter to the
   constructor of ParallelThread_2, so that the new
   thread will have a reference to its parent. */

```
pThread2 = new ParallelThread_2 (this);
```

/* The next three statements create and start a new
   thread from a class that implements Runnable. This
   technique provides the parent class (PrimaryClass)
   with references that allow access to the data and
   methods of the new instance of Parallel_3, p3, and
   also, access to the new thread's data and methods,
   pThread3, (e.g., pThread.start(), below). This is the
   cleanest way to do it — the task is accomplished by
   three consecutive unambiguous statements. */

```
p3 = new Parallel_3 (this);
pThread3 = new Thread (p3);
pThread3.start ();
```

/* The next two statements create and start a new thread
   from a class that extends Thread — the task is accomplished
   in two consecutive unambiguous statements. */

```
      pThread4 = new ParallelThread_4 (this);
      pThread4.start ();
   }
   private void stopThreads () {
      keepCounting = false; // Discontinue thread counting,
      try {
      Thread.sleep (100);   // but allow time to stop.
      }
      catch (InterruptedException e) {
      System.out.println ("Main thread interrupted");
      }
```

/* Next, since the Primary class has no reference to
   \ipThread1\c, and thus, can't invoke the stop() method
   of the Thread class, it uses a reference to Parallel_1,
   \ip1\c, to call the stop() method of the Parallel_1
   class. Note: Because Parallel_1 implements Runnable,
   there are two associated objects: p1, the instance of
   the class, and pThread1, the instance of the thread. */

```
      p1.stop ();
```

// Stop the other three threads from running.

```
      pThread2.stop ();
      pThread3.stop ();
      pThread4.stop ();
   }
   public static void main (String args []) {
```

/* The first statement of the main() method creates an
   instance of the primary class, pc, so main() will have
   a reference to its members. Note: Since the class name
   (PrimaryClass) appears on the left of the object
   creation statement, pc is technically a local variable,
   but it doesn't matter — the entire application is local
   to the main() method. */

```
      PrimaryClass pc = new PrimaryClass ();
      pc.spinOffThreads ();
```

```
  try {
    Thread.sleep (1000); // Allow time for counting
  }
  catch (InterruptedException e) {
  System.out.println ("Main thread interrupted");
  }
  pc.stopThreads ();
  try {
  System.out.print (
    '\n' + "Thread counter 1 = " + pc.ctr1 +
    '\n' + "Thread counter 2 = " + pc.ctr2 +
    '\n' + "Thread counter 3 = " + pc.ctr3 +
    '\n' + "Thread counter 4 = " + pc.ctr4 +
    '\n' );
  }
  catch (Exception e) { System.exit (1); }
  System.exit (2);        // Exit main thread
  }
}


class Parallel_1 implements Runnable {
  PrimaryClass parent;
  Thread pThread1;
  Parallel_1 (PrimaryClass Parent) {
    parent = Parent;        // Needs reference to parent
  }

/* Following are two references to start() methods: (1)
  the start() method defined in this class — the name
  start() is by convention, and (2) the call to the
  start() method of the Thread class (9 lines down).
  Note: The call to the Thread start() method must be
  qualified by the name of the thread object,
  \ipThread1\c, since Parallel_1 cannot directly access
  Thread methods, since it implements Runnable. */

  void start () {

/* The next line creates an instance of a thread by
  passing a runnable object, this, to the Thread
```

constructor. The this keyword refers to the current
object. */

```
  pThread1 = new Thread (this);
  pThread1.start ();  // The Thread start() method
                      // will initiate parallel
                      // execution of run().
}
public void run ()     // Parallel code must appear here.
{
  while (true) {
  if (parent.keepCounting) parent.ctr1++;
  }
}
```

```
/* The following stop() method, defined by the programmer,
   will invoke the stop() method of the Thread object —
   \ipThread1\c. */

  public void stop () {
    pThread1.stop (); // Stop pThread1 from running
  }
}
```

```
class ParallelThread_2 extends Thread {
  PrimaryClass parent;
  ParallelThread_2 (PrimaryClass Parent) {
    parent = Parent; // Needs reference to parent
```

```
/* The start() method of the Thread class is called.
   Since ParallelThread_2 has direct access to Thread
   methods (extends thread), no qualifier is necessary.
   However, it is generally not good programming practice
   to use the constructor of the Thread subclass to
   invoke start(). */

    start ();          // The Thread start() method will
                       // initiate parallel execution of
                       // run().
  }
  public void run ()   // Parallel code must appear here.
```

```
  {
    while (true)
    if (parent.keepCounting) parent.ctr2++;
  }
}

class Parallel_3 implements Runnable {
  PrimaryClass parent;
  Parallel_3 (PrimaryClass Parent) {
    parent = Parent; // Needs reference to parent
  }
  public void run () // Parallel code must appear here.
  {
    while (true)
    if (parent.keepCounting) parent.ctr3++;
  }
}

class ParallelThread_4 extends Thread {
  PrimaryClass parent;
  ParallelThread_4 (PrimaryClass Parent) {
    parent = Parent; // Needs reference to parent
  }
  public void run () // Parallel code must appear here.
  {
    while (true)
    if (parent.keepCounting) parent.ctr4++;
  }
}
```

The above example includes enough comments that it should be self-explanatory, but a few remarks are still worth making. Since the terms *instance*, *object*, *reference*, and *reference variable* were used in the previous example, it is probably a good place to review what these terms mean. An object is either an instance of a class, or an array. A reference variable contains a reference to an object. For example, when an instance of a class (e.g., Parallel_3) is created, the reference variable, p3, contains a reference to that object. Even though it is technically more precise to refer to p3 as a reference variable, usually the name of a reference variable is used as if it is the name of the object itself (e.g., declare p3 as an object). There is a good reason for this: An object has no name other than the name (or names) of the reference variable (or variables) that refer to it. Reference variables are also referred to in their more precise context (e.g., `parent1` provides a reference to the parent).

When the second through the fourth threads were created in the `spinOffThreads()` method, the object declaration part could have been left out, like it had been when the first thread was created. This would have avoided the hassle of reassigning the objects to non-local reference variables. For threads created utilizing the `Runnable` interface, it is clearer to create and start the thread with three consecutive statements. For threads created from a Thread subclass, two consecutive statements is the best. A useful method to remember when doing this is `currentThread()`. For example, to suspend the current thread,

```
Thread.currentThread().suspend()
```

can be used in a class that doesn't have a reference to its own thread, such as `Parallel_3`.

Aside from what was described in this section, threads have other capabilities. Threads can be named, grouped, prioritized, allowed to continue running after the program has exited (Daemon threads), and added to, or deleted from, existing thread groups. A more complete description of the methods and fields of the Thread class is found in Chapter 5.

Java Class Libraries

The Java class libraries offer a rich programming resource. The extensive functionality contained in the Java library packages can be used directly by creating instances of library classes, and then calling their methods. Or individual classes can be modified to fit a specific situation. Either way, the programmer doesn't have to reinvent the wheel.

5.1 The `java.lang` Package

The Object class, which resides in the `java.lang` package, in effect is the apex of the pyramid that is formed by the entire class libraries. Much of the `java.lang` package, such as the Thread, String, and System classes, have been covered in earlier chapters. Table 5.1 includes the more important classes and interfaces found in the `java.lang` package.

TABLE 5.1
Classes and Interfaces in `java.lang`

Class/Interface	Description
Boolean	Provides an object wrapper for the `boolean` data type.
Character	Provides an object wrapper for the `char` data type.
Class	For each class, Java maintains a class object which contains the class name, the class it extends, interfaces it implements, and the loader used to load the class.
Cloneable	An interface that must be implemented by any object that can be cloned.
Error	The superclass of all nonrecoverable error classes.
Exception	The superclass of all recoverable error classes.
Math	Contains methods for math functions such as trigonometric functions, absolute value, etc.
Number	Contains methods to retrieve the wrapped value as a `byte`, a `short`, an `int`, a `long`, a `float`, or a `double`.
Object	The root class. If a program does not explicitly state which class it extends, it extends `Object`.
Process	An abstract class. A `Process` object provides communication with a system program (usually an operating system and written in the system's native language).

TABLE 5.1 (Continued)

Class/Interface	Description
Runnable	The `Runnable` interface is implemented by the Thread class and by user-defined threads that do not extend the Thread class.
Runtime	An abstract class that handles the running of SecurityManager external programs. A security manager enforces policies as to what a program is allowed to do. A Web browser will define a security manager to prevent downloaded applets from accessing local files.
String	Provides methods for manipulating Java strings.
StringBuffer	Each time a string is appended, a new `String` object is created. A `StringBuffer` is more efficient because a single object can be appended one or more times, then assigned to a String object.
System	The System class provides special system level functions. Examples include I/O from and to standard I/O devices, memory management, and the definition of the security manager.
Thread	The Thread class includes methods to control the execution state of `thread`. A thread can be created by extending the Thread class or by passing to a `Thread` constructor an object of a class that implements the `Runnable` interface.
Throwable	The superclass of all error and exception classes.

The Int, Long, Float, and Double classes, not shown in Table 5.1, are subclasses of the Number class. The Number class, along with the Char and Boolean classes are referred to as *wrappers*. Wrappers are used to work around the fact that primitive data types are not objects. For example, the `java.util.HashTable` class cannot work with primitive data types. If a hashtable of integers were implemented using `HashTable`, int values would be wrapped in `Int` objects prior to being stored in the hashtable.

5.1.1 Thread Class

An important class of the `java.lang` package is the Thread class. Table 5.2 lists some useful Thread methods and describes what they do.

TABLE 5.2
Member Summary of Thread Class

Field or Method	Description
getName()	Returns name of current thread
getPriority()	Returns priority of current thread
getThreadGroup()	Returns group of current thread
isDaemon()	Returns true if current thread is Daemon
setDaemon()	Sets current thread to Daemon status
setName()	Assigns name to current thread
setPriority()	Assigns priority to current thread
MAX_PRIORITY	Maximum priority on current system
MIN_PRIORITY	Minimum priority on current system
destroy()	Destroys thread without cleanup

TABLE 5.2 (continued)

resume()	Resumes execution after suspension
sleep()	Puts thread to sleep for specified period
start()	Causes run() method to execute
suspend()	Suspends thread's execution
yield()	Causes currently executing thread to yield to another thread

5.2 The `java.awt` Package

The `java.awt` package provides the programmer with the capability to define a Graphical User Interface (GUI) complete with windows, pop-up menus, scrollbars, textfields, and buttons. The Abstract Windowing Toolkit (AWT) contains all the classes needed to build hierarchies of graphical components for GUI's. Figure 5.1 shows the structure of the Component superclass and its subclasses, which give the programmer the flexibility to create customized GUI's.

The Component class and one of its subclasses, the Container class, are abstract classes that cannot be instantiated. However, their methods, and therefore their basic functionality, are inherited by all their subclasses.

A *container* is a special kind of component that can contain other components. Instances of the Window, Panel, Frame, and Dialog classes are containers, but they are also components (see Figure 5.1). To give a general idea of how this works, a window could contain a textarea component and a panel component (perhaps covering the top three quarters and bottom quarter of the window, respectively). Since a panel is also a container, the panel could contain additional components, perhaps a button, a label, and a textfield. This would allow the user two ways of making something happen in the window—by using a mouse to push the button, or by entering text in the textfield or textarea. Figure 5.2 shows a popup window used to find a file's location(s).

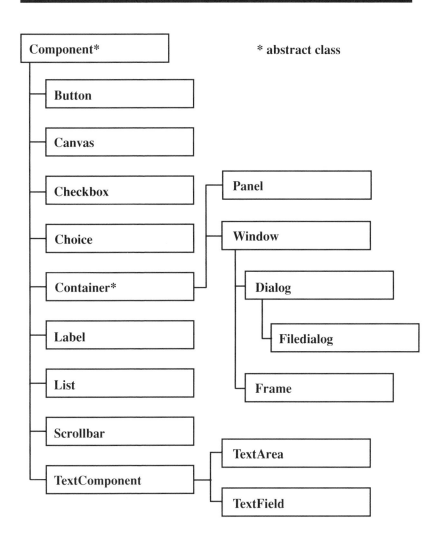

Figure 5.1 Component Hierarchy

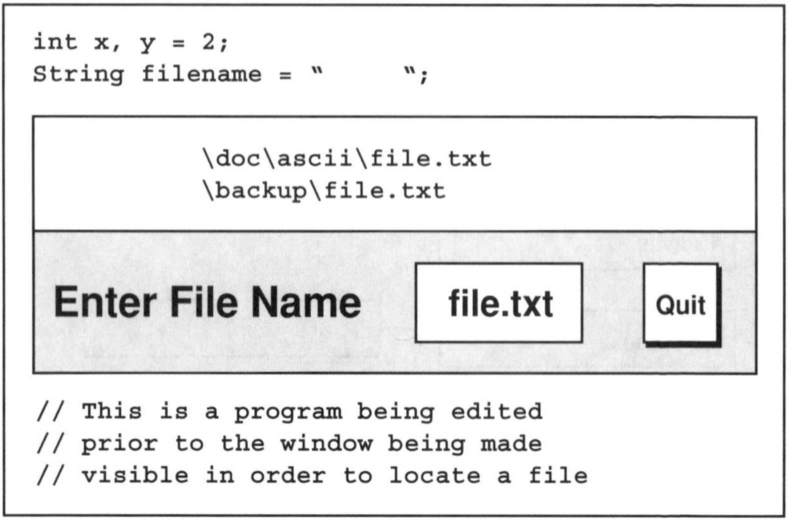

```
int x, y = 2;
String filename = "      ";
```

```
              \doc\ascii\file.txt
              \backup\file.txt
```

Enter File Name   **file.txt**   Quit

```
// This is a program being edited
// prior to the window being made
// visible in order to locate a file
```

Figure 5.2 Popup Window

The panel of the popup window, in Figure 5.2, contains the label "Enter File Name", a textfield for entering the file name, and a quit button to make the window disappear. The popup window's text area contains the directories where the file name is located.

A window may be modal or modaless. If it is modal, when the window is visible only the window's components will respond to an "event," for example a mouse click or a keystroke. If it is modaless, components outside the window will also respond to events. A frame (see Figure 5.1) is a special type of window that has these additional properties:

1. **Title Bar**: A title bar is a strip across the top of the frame that can be used for a short description of what the frame does.

2. **Icon**: The title bar includes an icon that allows the frame to be iconified.

3. **Menu Bar**: A frame is the only type of container that can add a menu bar.

4. **Redefinable Cursor**: By default, the cursor is an arrow, but can be redefined by a frame object to a variety of sizes and shapes.

5. **Resizability**: A frame's horizontal and vertical dimensions can be changed.

6. **Border**: A frame has a border. The default thickness of the border can be altered by calling the `Container.insets()` method.

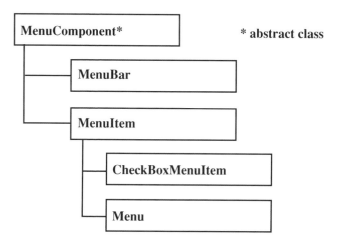

Figure 5.3 `MenuComponent` **Hierarchy**

Figure 5.3 shows the structure of the `MenuComponent` superclass and its subclasses. The frame is the only container that can add a menu bar. Once a menu bar has been added to a frame, the methods of not only the Frame class, but also the methods of superclasses of Frame, such as Component and Container, can be used to respond to menu events. For example, assume a menu bar contains the word "File" and the word "Edit." If the user clicked on "File," a drop-down menu would appear. Then, if the user proceeds to click on one of the items of the "File" menu, the program can use either the `handleEvent()` method or the `processEvent()` method of the Component class to process the event. Event processing is explained in the next two sections.

5.2.1 The Java 1.0 Event Model

The Java 1.0 event model, which was deprecated beginning with version 1.1, relies on overriding the `handleEvent()` method of the Component class (see below). Since it is still found in a lot of existing code, it is handy to know the 1.0 event model, but it is incompatible with the event handling introduced in Java 1.1. Although the `handleEvent()` method is still included in Java 1.1, the programmer should be careful not to mix the two event models.

In Java version 1.0, when an event occurs, an `Event` object—an instance of the `java.awt.Event` class—is generated. Then, the `java.awt` invokes the `handleEvent()` method of the source component. For example, if a button is pressed, the `handleEvent()` method of that particular button is invoked. Since the Button class extends the Component class, it has a `handleEvent()` method by inheritance. A programmer who wants to handle events generated by a button at the level of the button component will normally override the `action()` method, shown below. This is because a pressed button generates an `ACTION_EVENT`. An alternative way to process an event at the button level is to override either the `mouseDown()` or `mouseUp()` method. These methods also will work because buttons generate `MOUSE_DOWN` and `MOUSE_UP` events if the mouse is clicked on them.

```
public boolean handleEvent (Event evt) {
  switch (evt.id) {
    case Event.MOUSE_ENTER:
      return mouseEnter (evt, evt.x, evt.y);
    case Event.MOUSE_EXIT:
      return mouseExit (evt, evt.x, evt.y);
    case Event.MOUSE_MOVE:
      return mouseMove (evt, evt.x, evt.y):
    case Event.MOUSE_DOWN:
      return mouseDown (evt, evt.x, evt.y);
    case Event.MOUSE_DRAG:
      return mouseDrag (evt, evt.x, evt.y);
```

```
    case Event.MOUSE_UP:
      return mouseUp (evt, evt.x, evt.y);
    case Event.KEY_PRESS:
    case Event.KEY_ACTION:
      return keyDown (evt, evt.key);
    case Event.KEY_RELEASE:
    case Event.KEY_ACTION_RELEASE:
      return keyUp (evt, evt.key);
    case Event.ACTION_EVENT:
      return action (evt, evt.arg);
    case Event.GOT_FOCUS:
      return gotFocus (evt, evt.arg)'
    case Event.LOST_FOCUS:
      return lostFocus (evt, evt.arg);
  }
  return false;
}
```

The evt parameter of the handleEvent() method above is an in-stance of the Event class. The evt object is generated by Java in response to an operating system event. A GUI can be made responsive to user events (a mouse movement or click, or a keystroke) by overriding handleEvent() or one of the method calls in its switch statement.

The highest level container of an application is most often a frame. The frame may contain components such as a textfield, or the frame may contain other containers, such as a panel. The panel may contain components, such as a button, or yet another container. The whole thing forms a hierarchy with the highest level container referred to as the *parent* of its components, which are its *children*. The highest level container is referred to as the *ancestor* of its children's children.

If a frame contained a panel which contained a button, the button would be considered a relatively low-level component. If an application wanted to respond to a button event (e.g., the button being pushed by a user clicking a mouse), it could override the low-level component's (the button's) handleEvent() method. However, Java allows all events to traverse up the component hierarchy, so they can be intercepted by the highest level component's (the frame's) handleEvent() method.

5.2.2 The Java 1.1 Event Model

It may sound contradictory, but the biggest advantage of the Java 1.0 event model has also turned out to be what has caused the most problems—especially for complex applications. Because Java 1.0 allows events to be handled at the top of the containment hierarchy, the programmer does not, for example, have to create a customized button just to process a single action event. But unfortunately, if the program is designed to process all events in a top level Frame class, the event handling code can get pretty convoluted. Individual software components (objects) should be as self-contained as possible, so they can be tested and debugged separately. Also, not only objects, but even methods, that are members of the same class should still be as removable and replaceable as possible—thus facilitating code reuse.

The Java 1.1 event model is based on the concept of the event listener. Unlike Java 1.0, which relies on a single `Event` object and a single processing method (`handleEvent()`), Java 1.1 defines a separate `AWTEvent` subclass for each kind of event and a separate listener interface to process each `AWTEvent`. The source of the event, usually a component, notifies a listener when an event has occurred. It does this by invoking the appropriate listener method, with the method's parameter being an instance of an `AWTEvent` subclass.

Figure 5.4 shows the class and interface structure of the `java.awt.event` package. All event (ending in `Event`) classes extend the `AWTEvent` class of the `java.awt` package (not shown); all adapter (ending in `Adapter`) classes extend the Object class of the `java.lang` package (not shown), and all listener (ending in `Listener`) interfaces extend the `EventListener` interface of the `java.util` package (not shown).

As shown in Figure 5.4, the `java.awt.event` package provides a corresponding listener interface for every event class—actually two in the case of `MouseEventClass`: `MouseMotionListener` and `MouseListener`. For every event potentially generated by an

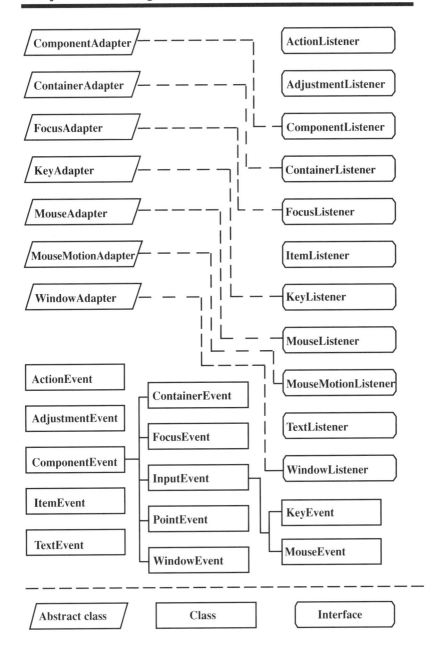

Figure 5.4 The java.awt.event Package

application's (or applet's) GUI, the programmer must define an event listener. This is done in one of two ways: (1) by implementing the appropriate listener interface, or, (2) if an adapter class exists for that event (see dotted lines in Figure 5.4), by subclassing the adapter class. Abstract adapter classes implement listener interfaces, but do not define method bodies. The idea of adapter classes is that, if only some of the listener's methods are required, it is less work to subclass the adapter—overriding only the listener methods actually needed. The `java.awt.event` interfaces that have no corresponding adapter class contain only one method.

The listener object registers itself with the source component by invoking methods that take the form `addEventListener` (e.g., `addActionEventListener`). The following code segment shows how a `TextEventListener` might inform a text component that it wants to be notified of `TextEvents`:

```
class TextClass implements TextEventListener {
    . . .
  /*  Code that implements TextEventListener methods
      (to be explained later). */
    . . .
  /*  In this example, the main() method, which is part of
      TextClass, will register the TextEventListener. */
  public static void main (String args []) {
  /*  main() first creates an instance of the class that
      implements the TextEventListener, the current
      class, in this example. */
  TextClass tc;  tc = new TextClass ();
        // Then main() creates an instance of the source
  TextArea ta; ta = new TextArea ();
  /*  Next, the Listener object, tc, is registered with
      the source component, ta, so the listener methods
      will be notified of any TextEvent. */
  ta.addTextEventListener (tc);
    . . .
  }
}
```

Table 5.3 presents the Java 1.1 AWTEvents, the public methods of each event class, and the methods required to implement each listener interface.

TABLE 5.3
AWTEvent Classes and Listener Interfaces

	Events	**Listener**
Class/Interface	ActionEvent	ActionListener
Public Methods	getModifiers() getActionCommand()[1]	actionPerformed()
Class/Interface	AdjustmentEvent	AdjustmentListener()
Public Methods	getAdjustable()[1] getAdjustmentType() getValue()	adjustmentValue- Changed()
Class/Interface	ComponentEvent	ComponentListener
Public Methods	getComponent()[1]	ComponentHidden() ComponentMoved() ComponentResized() ComponentShown()
Class/Interface	ContainerEvent	ContainerListener
Public Methods	getChild() getContainer()[1]	componentAdded() componentRemoved()
Class/Interface	FocusEvent	FocusListener
Public Methods	isTemporary()	focusGained() focusLost()
Class/Interface	ItemEvent	ItemListener

Public Methods	getItem() getItemSelectable()[1] getStateChange()	itemStateChanged()
Class/Interface	KeyEvent	KeyListener
Public Methods	getKeyCode() getKeyChar() isAction()	keyPressed() keyReleased() keyTyped()
Class/Interface	MouseEvent	MouseListener
Public Methods	getClickCount() getPoint() getX() getY()	mouseClicked() mouseEntered() mouseExited() mousePressed() mouseReleased()
Class/Interface	MouseEvent	MouseMotion-Listener
Public Methods	getClickCount() getPoint() getX() getY()	mouseDragged() mouseMoved()
Class/Interface	TextEvent	TextListener
Public Methods		textValueChanged()
Class/Interface	WindowEvent	WindowListener
Public Methods	getWindow()[1]	windowActivated() windowClosed() windowClosing() windowDeactivated() windowDeiconified() windowIconified() windowOpened()

[1] Alternative to getSource()

All of the AWTEvent subclasses inherit the `getId()` method from the AWTEvent class. The `getId()` method can be used to determine the event type. For example, the `ActionListener` interface could be implemented as shown below:

```
actionPerformed (ActionEvent e) {
  if (e.getId() == e.ACTION_PERFORMED) {
    if (e.getActionCommand() == "Display Text") {
      code to display text
    }
  }
}
```

Whenever the `actionPerformed()` listener method is invoked, the id is always ACTION_PERFORMED, so the use of the `getId()` method shown above is actually superfluous. Similarly, in the case of the MouseMotion listener, if the `mouseClicked()` method is invoked, the id is always MOUSE_CLICKED, and if the `mousePressed()` method is invoked, the id is always MOUSE_PRESSED. In fact, for any event type the id is implicitly known by the listener method. The `getId()` is still available, however, either for purposes of style, or for unusual cases.

The `getActionCommand()` method utilized in the above `ActionListener` interface returns a name that was earlier assigned to a button or a menu item. If no name was assigned, `getActionCommand()` returns the String value of the label of the button or menu item. The source of the `ActionEvent` can also be determined by the `getSource()` method, which is inherited from the EventObject class—the superclass of AWTEvent. For example:

```
actionPerformed (ActionEvent e) {
  if (e.getSource() instanceof TextField) {
    TextField tf = e.getSource();
    String txt = tf.getText();
    // code to process new text
  }
    // more if statements (to process other action events)
}
```

Most AWTEvents define alternative methods to `getSource()` (see Table 5.3). The events generated by the different source components are presented in Table 5.4.

TABLE 5.4
Events Generated by Different Source Components

Event Generated	Component	Meaning
ActionEvent	Button	Button clicked on by user.
	List	Double click on list item.
	MenuItem	Menu item selected by user.
	TextField	User pressed enter while editing text field.
AdjustmentEvent	Scrollbar	Scrollbar moved by user.
ComponentEvent	Component	Component resized, hidden, moved, or shown.
ContainerEvent	Container	Component added or removed.
FocusEvent	Component	Focus gained or lost.
ItemEvent	CheckBox	Item selected or deselected.
	CheckBoxMenuItem	Item selected or deselected.
	Choice	Item selected or deselected.
	List	Item selected or deselected.
KeyEvent	Component	Key pressed or released by user.
MouseEvent	Component	Mouse moved, dragged, pressed, released, or entered or exited component.

TextEvent	TextComponent	Text changed by user
WindowEvent	Window	Window opened, closed, iconified, or deiconified

Low Level Java 1.3 Event Processing

When a component generates an event, the processEvent() method of that component is invoked by the AWT. The processEvent() method in turn invokes methods specific to that type of event. For example, a key event will cause processEvent() to invoke the processKeyEvent() method, and an action event will cause processEvent() to invoke the processActionEvent() method. Since programs that use the 1.3 event model usually implement listener interfaces, by default the specific event methods simply dispatch the event to the registered listeners. However, 1.3 model events can be processed analogously to the 1.0 model (referred to as "low level event processing"). This is done by first enabling the events the programmer wants to be processed at a low level, as shown:

```
enableEvents (AWTEvent.ACTION_EVENT_MASK |
    AWTEvent.KEY_EVENT_MASK);
```

ACTION_EVENT_MASK and KEY_EVENT_MASK are two 64-bit constants. An OR operation is operated on them to produce another bit mask that specifies the events to be intercepted. Next, the programmer can either override all of processEvent, or only specific methods such as processActionEvent(). The names of these specific methods take the form: processXXXEvent() where XXX is the name of the event class (Figure 5.4). The one case when the previous rule does not hold is that a MouseEvent object may be processed by either processMouseEvent() or processMouseMotionEvent(). The names of the event mask constants take the form XXX_EVENT_MASK where XXX is the all uppercase name of the event class, with one exception: MOUSE_MOTION_EVENT_MASK, which does not have a corresponding event class. Events are further discussed in Section 7.2 Processing Application Program Events.

5.2.3 The LayoutManager Interface

The java.awt.LayoutManager interface defines abstract methods to facilitate laying out individual components within a container. Four commonly used classes that implement the LayoutManager interface are described below:

1. **FlowLayout:** This class provides methods that automatically lay out components from left to right and from top to bottom, in the order they are added. If a component cannot fit in a row without being clipped, a new row is added. The flow layout is the most intuitive layout manager, and is the default layout for Panel and Applet containers.

2. **BorderLayout:** The border layout is the default layout of a Frame. The BorderLayout class provides methods that allow up to five components to be added near the left border, near the right border, near the top, near the bottom, and in the center of a container. For example, the following seven statements would cause buttons to be added near the top and bottom of a frame, and a text area to be added in its center:

```
Frame fr = new Frame ();
Button topBtn = new Button ("Top");
Button lowBtn = new Button ("Bottom");
TextArea ta = new TextArea ();
fr.add (topBtn, BorderLayout.NORTH);
fr.add (lowBtn, BorderLayout.SOUTH);
fr.add (ta, BorderLayout.CENTER);
```

3. **GridLayout**: This class divides the container into a specified number of rows and columns (a grid) and places the components within the grid, left to right, and top to bottom.

4. **GridBagLayout**: Provides the methods to place components within a grid whose compartments may not necessarily have the same width or height. The most flexible, and most complicated, of the layout managers.

The layout manager for a container, other than the default layout manager, can be specified by the setLayout() method. For example:

```
Frame gf = new Frame ();        // Frame default layout
                                // manager is BorderLayout.
gf.setLayout (GridLayout());    // But it can be made a
                                // GridLayout.
```

5.2.4 AWT Component Graphics

To a great extent, the AWT handles the details of a GUI for the programmer. However, programmers who want to draw their own images, or create their own text, must utilize the methods of the Graphics class. A Graphics object can be obtained by the getGraphics() method of the Component class, for example:

```
class AnyFrame extends Frame {
int upperLeftX = 50, upperLeftY = 50, width =15, height = 20;
                    // Rest of field declarations go here
  ...
  void drawMethod () {
  Graphics g = getGraphics();
                    // Gets graphics object of frame
  g.drawString ("Any string", 100, 100);
                    // Draws with current font
  g.drawRect (UpperLeftX, UpperLeftY, width, height);
                    // Current foreground color
  }
  ...
}
```

Other useful methods of the Graphics class include:

```
drawLine (int x1, int y1, int x2, int y2);
drawPolygon (int [] xPts, int [] yPts, int nbrPts);
fillPolygon (int [] xPts, int [] yPts, nbrPts);
drawImage (Image image, int x, int y, ImageObserver
                                        observer);
                    // e.g., GIF image
setFont (Font font);
setColor (Color color);
```

The Paint() Method of the Component Class

Programmers can "paint" (draw images and text) their own window, in effect creating their own component. Or they can paint part of a window by including a Canvas object as one of the components that fill up a container. Whether all, or part, of a window, is painted by the application programmer, the `paint()` method of the Component class needs to be overridden. There are two reasons that necessitate this. The first is that the AWT calls `paint()` to make a component visible, and the second is that when a component is damaged by another window temporarily popping up in front of it, the AWT calls `repaint()`. The `repaint()` method, in turn, invokes `paint()` to do the redrawing. Applets are usually good examples of overriding `paint()`, because they do a lot of their own drawing (see Chapter 6 Applets).

One of the points of confusion regarding the `paint()` method is that the programmer does not have to provide a graphics context. For example:

```
public void paint (Graphics g) {
/* Method of the Graphics class usually go here, e.g.,
   drawLine(). */
}
```

A `paint()` method with the above general outlines can be used to draw and refresh a window without the window class containing any code to create a graphics context (i.e., the `getGraphics()` method). It almost seems like the Graphics object g magically appears, but what happens is that when the AWT invokes `paint()` it supplies the component's graphics context, or if the component does not have one, a graphics context with default values for foreground color, background color, and font is supplied.

5.3 The `java.net` Package

A Java program can communicate with any server on the Internet. The `java.net` package also may be used by an organization to develop their own internet. Despite its other innovations and capabilities, the rapid acceptance of Java is due to its powerful integration with the Internet and the World Wide Web.

In this section we will concentrate on two high-level communication interfaces: (1) *sockets*, and (2) *uniform resource locators* (URLs). The following is a brief description of some of the more important classes of the `java.net` package:

1. **Socket**: The TCP/IP (Internet) protocol suite provides the rules of communication between computers on an internet. The Socket class provides an interface between the application program and the underlying TCP/IP, which frees the programmer from being concerned with the protocol's details.

2. **SocketServer**: A *server* computer may provide services for several *client* computers simultaneously. The ServerSocket class helps to provide an interface between a server program and the underlying TCP/IP (Internet) protocol.

3. **InetAddress**: A host computer on an internet can be identified by both a name and an address. A host computer has only one name, but may have more than one address. An InetAddress object contains a host's name and address(es). The InetAddress class includes methods for obtaining the address(es) of the local host, or a remote host.

4. **URL**: A Uniform Resource Locator is a descriptor of how to locate a resource on the Internet. An instance of the URL class consists of a copy of a URL descriptor, methods that will return the individual components of that descriptor, and methods that will obtain the remote resource identified by the URL descriptor.

5. **URLConnection**: The URLConnection class is used to establish a much more flexible connection to a resource identified by a URL. A URLConnection allows options such as activating a memory cache, allowing user interaction, and encoding user information into the URL descriptor. The URLConnection class is an abstract class, and as such cannot be instantiated. However, a URLConnection object can be created by calling the `openConnection()` method of the URL class.

5.3.1 Sockets

A socket is the endpoint of a communications link. Sockets can be used to implement client-server, or peer-to-peer communication. The concept of the socket was originally developed at the University of California at Berkeley for the UNIX operating system, but has since been implemented on computers with a wide variety of operating systems.

TCP Sockets

There are two types of sockets implemented on an internet: TCP sockets and UDP sockets (also part of TCP/IP). Although the Socket class is an abstraction intended to hide the protocol's implementation, some understanding of the TCP/IP protocol suite is helpful.

The Internet, whose rules of communication are provided by TCP/IP, is the premier global network. An internet is a TCP/IP network whose host computers are not on the Internet. The Transport Control Protocol (TCP) is responsible for handling end-system to end-system communication. The Internet Protocol (IP) is responsible for routing "packets" across the network. Every host on an internet has a unique IP address.

Host computers are identified by IP addresses, but the TCP completes the identifier by adding a *port number*, which is used to differentiate between applications with the same IP address. Servers accept connections from multiple clients on *well-known* ports. These well-known ports represent commonly used application protocols, some of which are shown in Table 5.5.

TABLE 5.5
Common Application Protocols

Port	Application Protocol	Service
21	FTP	File Transfer Protocol –file transfer
23	TELNET	Terminal emulator
25	SMTP	Internet mail transfer
80	HTTP	Hyper-Text Markup Language – commonly used for transferring URLs.

The above port numbers are said to be "bound" to server applications. Client applications must also "bind" a port number in order to establish a socket connection, however client applications can only bind what are called *ephemeral* ports—those above 1024.

Java requires four pieces of information in order to create a TCP socket:

1. The Internet address of the local system.

2. The local application's TCP port number.

3. The Internet address of the remote system.

4. The remote application's TCP port number.

More than one client may be served on a TCP server port, however, no more than one server application may be bound to the same port. This results in a unique identifier for every socket. Figure 5.5 shows an example of IP addresses and port numbers that would result in a unique identifier for each TCP socket. Note: This system would have six sockets—one for each communication end-point.

One thing that is not shown in Figure 5.5 is that although a host computer is identified by no more than one name, it sometimes has more than one IP address. This is because each *wire*, or physical connection, has to be uniquely identified. The InetAddress class can be used to store and obtain the Internet address(es) of a local or remote host, as shown in the following code segment:

```
String hostName = "www.javasoft.com";
InetAddress localInetAddr, remoteInetAddr,
InetAddress remoteInetAddrs [];
try {
  localInetAddr =
    InetAddress.getLocalHost ();
  remoteInetAddr =
    InetAddress.getByName (hostName);
  remoteInetAddrs =
    InetAddress.getAllByName (hostName);
}
catch (UnknownHostException e) {
  System.err.println ("Unknown host exception");
}
```

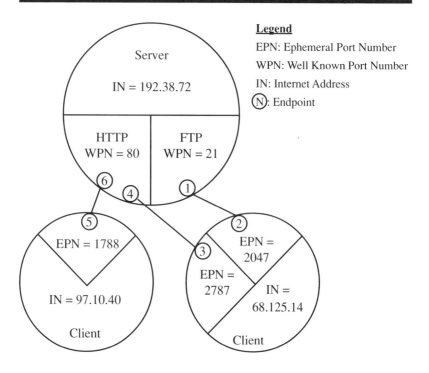

Figure 5.5 Sockets

Sockets				
Endpoint	Local Port #	Remote Port #	Local Internet Address	Remote Internet Address
1	21	2047	192.38.72	68.125.14
2	2047	21	68.125.14	192.38.72
3	2787	80	68.125.14	192.38.72
4	80	2787	192.38.72	68.125.14
5	1788	80	97.10.40	192.38.72
6	80	1788	192.38.72	97.10.40

A TCP connection with a remote host is established by means of the Socket constructor. Although a socket requires four pieces of information, it isn't always necessary to provide the local address and port number. The local address is already known by Java and an unused ephemeral port number will be automatically selected. However, there are cases where the programmer will want to customize the interface by providing the local address and port number; for example, if a local host has more than one IP address. The Socket constructor has four forms:

```
public Socket (String remoteHost, int remotePort) throws
   UnknownHostException, IOException;
public Socket (InetAddress remoteAddr, int remotePort)
   throws IOException;
public Socket (String remoteHost, int remotePort,
   InetAddress localAddr, int localPort) throws
   UnknownHostException, IOException;
public Socket (InetAddress remoteHost, int remotePort,
   InetAddress localAddr, int localPort) throws
   UnknownHostException, IOException;
```

Once a TCP socket connection is established, it is necessary to create stream objects in order to read and write data. InputStream and OutputStream objects can be created by calling the Socket class's `getInputStream()` and `getOutputStream()` methods. These basic streams are usually "decorated" by feeding them through I/O streams with filtering capability. This technique is illustrated below:

```
Socket netCom = new Socket ("www.javasoft.com", 21);
DataInputStream netIn =
   new DataInputStream (netCom.getInputStream());
DataOutputStream dataOut =
   new DataOutputStream (netCom.getOntputStream());
PrintStream netOut =
   new PrintStream (dataOut);
```

The ServerSocket class provides the means for a TCP server application to accept connection requests from multiple clients. When a ServerSocket object is created, it is bound to a well-known port. The ServerSocket object then enters a "listening" state in which it keeps track of client connect requests. The ServerSocket constructor has three forms:

```
public ServerSocket (int wellKnownPort) throws IOException;
```

```
public ServerSocket (int wellKnownPort, int queLimit)
   throws IOException;
public ServerSocket (int wellKnownPort, int queLimit,
   InetAddress localInetAddr) throws IOException;
```

The first ServerSocket constructor's only parameter is the well-known port number. However, while it is in the listening state, up to fifty clients (the default number) will be queued, pending a complete socket connection. If a client requests a connection when the server queue is full, it will result in an IOException being thrown on the client system. The second constructor includes a parameter for the queue limit. The third constructor allows a server application to customize the interface by specifying the IP address. After a ServerSocket is created the accept() method can be used to connect an individual client. The accept() method blocks until a client connects, then returns a Socket object, as shown below:

```
import java.io.*;
import java.net.*;
     . . .
try {
   ServerSocket server = new ServerSocket (23);
   Socket client = server.accept();
   }
catch (IOException e) {
   System.err.println ("Unknown client exception");
}
      . . .
/* Code to open I/O streams to socket, communicate
   with client, then to close I/O streams. */
      . . .
   client.close();  // Disconnect socket
```

Most server applications are quite complex, with the above example being an over-simplification. Usually there is either a long-running or an infinite loop (perhaps part of a concurrently executing thread) that accepts numerous connections from the same ServerSocket object. This same loop will usually include method calls to process those connections. When a client's communication is completed, the server closes the I/O streams, then the Socket.close() method is called to disconnect the socket, as shown above.

5.3.2 Uniform Resource Locators (URLs)

A URL is a string that describes how to locate and access a resource on the Internet. URLs were developed for Web browsers, but were made flexible enough to include applications that long preceded the Web.

Programs that use URLs operate at a higher level than programs that use sockets. Sockets provide an interface between an application and a TCP/IP network. This means that the socket programmer is, in effect, designing her own application level protocol. URLs allow the programmer to select a *scheme*. The scheme includes the specification of an *existing* application protocol. Thus, by providing an application protocol, URLs make the details of the underlying socket interface transparent to the programmer.

A URL is made up of the following components in the order listed:

1. **Scheme**: The scheme component (e.g., http, ftp, gopher, telnet, mailto, etc.) can be thought of as the specification of the Internet application protocol. However, selection of the scheme actually does more than specifying the protocol. For example, the URL "mailto://rfr@nethost.com" causes mail to be sent to user "rfr" at host "nethost.com". The URL "ftp://rfr@nethost.com/" causes the program to establish an FTP (File Transfer Protocol) connection at "nethost.com", and to log on as user "rfr".

2. **Host Name**: This component specifies the name of the host or domain to establish a connection with in order to access the resource (e.g., www.javasoft.com).

3. **Port Number**: The port number in most cases is well-known, so this component is optional. An example would be "ftp://rfr@nethost.com:21/". The port number for FTP (see Table 5.5) is known to be 21, so the port number and the ":" separator can be left out. In certain cases, however, it is necessary to specify a port number.

4. **File Name**: The file name component specifies the file name or the directory name where the resource is located on the remote host. A trailing slash indicates a directory. For example, in the URL "http://nethost.com/test/beta.doc", "/test/beta.doc" specifies

a file name. In the URL "ftp://nethost.com/test/", "/test/" specifies a directory name.

5. **Reference**: The reference component, which is optional, identifies the fragment of a document file to be accessed. The reference component is preceded by a "#". The URL "http://
nethost.com/test/beta.html#READFIRST" would cause the fragment of the "/test/beta.html" file beginning with <A
name=READFIRST> and ending with </A name> to be accessed.
Hypertext Markup Language (HTML) documents, by convention,
are stored in files with an .html extension. HTML will be covered in Chapter 6 Java Applets.

A Java program accesses a URL by first creating a URL object. The
URL class constructor has four forms:

```
public URL (String urlDescriptor) throws
   MalFormedURLException;
public URL (String scheme, String hostName,
   String fileName) throws
   MalFormedURLException;
public URL (String scheme, String hostName,
   int portNumber, String fileName) throws
   MalFormedURLException;
public URL (String urlObject, String newFileName)
   throws MalFormedURLException;
```

The most commonly used URL constructor is the first one. There is
no particular advantage to the second and third constructors, except, for
purposes of style, some programmers may prefer to specify the URL components individually. The fourth constructor conveniently allows a URL
object to be created from a previously defined URL by only altering the
file name. The last constructor is used often in applet programming, because the applet class returns the directory where the applet is stored.

The two most common techniques used to obtain useful data, once an
URL object has been created, are:

1. creating an InputStream object by calling the URL class's
   openStream() method, and

2. creating an URLConnection object by calling the URL class's openConnection() method.

If the first technique is used, the InputStream is usually decorated by feeding it through an I/O stream with filtering capability, as shown below:

```
import java.io.*
import java.net.*
    . . .
String inStr;         // Will hold a line of input
StringBuffer dataUrl; // Will hold all lines of input
try {
  URL netInfo =
    new URL ("ftp:     //www.nethost.com/data/info.txt");
    /* In next assignment statement, the openStream() method
       of the URL object (netInfo) creates an InputStream
       obj.*/
    DataInputStream netData =
       new DataInputStream (netInfo.openStream());
    inStr = netData.readLine();
    while (inStr != null) {   // Null means EOF
   /*info.txt assumed to be a small file, thus it isn't
     necessary for program to create a local file for
     it.*/
      dataUrl.append (inStr);
      inStr = netData.readLine();
         // readLine reads series of bytes &
  }        // returns a string.
}
catch (MalFormedURLException e)
  System.err.println ("Malformed URL");
catch (IOException e)
  System.err.println ("Input/Output error");
netData.close();
```

The URL class works fine for straightforward URL access such as the downloading of a small text file, or even a large GIF file. For much more flexible access the URLConnection class is available. The URLConnection class is abstract, but the URL class's openConnection() method can be used to create a URLConnection object. With a

URLConnection, both an InputStream and an OutputStream can be created, allowing interaction with the URL. Also, there are many more options such as specifying a search string with the number of hits returned by the URL. Unfortunately, the use of the URLConnnection class is very complex and beyond the scope of this book.

5.4 The `java.util` Package

The `java.util` package is an integral part of the Java language. The `util` package is basically made up of two parts. The first part consists of data structures: classes used for storing and retrieving collections of objects. The rest of the `util` package provides general utilities. The most commonly used classes are presented in Table 5.6.

TABLE 5.6
Data Structures Classes

Class	Description
Collection	An interface that defines methods for manipulating an unordered collection, or group, of objects. The objects may, or may not, contain duplicates.
Set	An interface that defines methods for manipulating a collection, or set of objects, or elements. The objects may, or may not, be ordered. A set may not contain duplicate objects.
List	An interface that can be implemented to manipulate an ordered collection of objects, or elements. A list may contain duplicate elements.

Map	An interface that represents a set of mappings between key objects and value objects (see HashTable).
AbstractCollection	An abstract implementation of Collection.
AbstractSet	An abstract implementation of Set.
AbstractList	An abstract implementation of List.
AbstractMap	An abstract implementation of Map.
HashTable	A class that can be used to store and retrieve key/value pairs. A key/value pair is a mapping, or an association, between a key object and a value object. Usually the key object is simpler, such as a name, while a value object is more complex, such as a whole employment record. The bucket in which the key/value pair is placed is determined by the hashCode() method, which returns a signed integer, an int.
HashMap	A map whose keys are kept in a hash table. A HashMap requires less overhead than a HashTable, but does not have synchronized methods. It is better to use HashTable for programs that require thread safety.
Enumeration	An interface that defines methods necessary to iterate through a set of values.
Vector	A commonly used java.util class. A vector is an expandable array of objects. The elements() method of Vector, which is synchronized, returns an enumeration. The nextElement() and hasMoreElements() methods of the Enumeration object can then be used to iterate through the vector's elements.

General Utilities	Description
Date	Returns date and time.
Random	Provides a pseudo random number generator.
StringTokenizer	This class is used to parse strings to sequences of tokens.

The discussion of the java.util package will be concluded with a few more words about how Java hash tables work. Since the Object class defines a hashCode() method, all objects have one, although many classes override hashCode(). An object's hash code is computed from its value. If hashCode() is overridden, then the class should also override the equals() method. For example, the Object class defines its value as its reference so that equals() and the "==" operators are equivalent, while the value of a Long object is the value of the long number it provides a wrapper for. Also, the programmer should be aware that while two key/value pairs may have duplicate value objects, the key may not be duplicated.

CHAPTER 6

Java Applets

The first thing that should be understood about applets is that every applet in the world extends the `java.applet.Applet` class. The Applet class—in terms of numbers of methods and fields—is a small class, and applets are usually small programs. However, the driving force behind Java's rapid acceptance is the widespread popularity of applets.

Applets are specialized panels which are embedded in specialized containers: Web browsers or applet viewers. Figure 6.1 shows the life cycle of an applet.

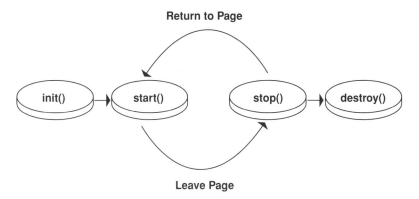

Figure 6.1 Applet States

The init(), start(), stop(), and destroy() methods are part of the Applet class and are invoked by the Web browser during the life cycle of the applet. If the applet scrolls off the Web page or if the browser goes to the next page, the applet is stopped from running by the browser invoking the stop() method. Later, if the applet reappears, the start() method is called.

Any one of the above methods can be overridden by the Applet subclass. The most important is the init() method, which functions as the de facto constructor. Although a constructor may be defined for an applet, there is little reason to have one because Web browsers do not pass parameters.

A Java application program can run from a command line, without bringing up a window, or it can provide a graphical user interface (GUI). If it provides a GUI, the main window is nearly always a frame, or in some cases a dialog box. In the case of applets, the main window is the applet itself and a GUI is always provided. There is actually a close relationship between applets and frames. This can be viewed in two ways: (1) as both being at the lowest level of the component hierarchy (see Figure 6.2(a)), or (2) as both being at the highest level of the event hierarchy (see Figure 6.2(b)). Events may be intercepted at lower levels (see the button and panel in Figure 6.2(b)), or they may be intercepted at the highest level—when they reach the main window (the applet or frame in Figure 6.2(b)).

An applet can easily be converted to a stand-alone application by implementing five simple steps:

1. Redefine the init() method as the class constructor.

2. Change the declaration of the primary class (the class containing the init() method) so that it extends the Frame class rather than the Applet class.

3. Redefine the start() method as the main method. There may not be a start() method, because if the programmer does not define one, the browser automatically invokes the applet super.start() method. In this case, a main method must be created, either within the frame class or within a class newly defined for that purpose.

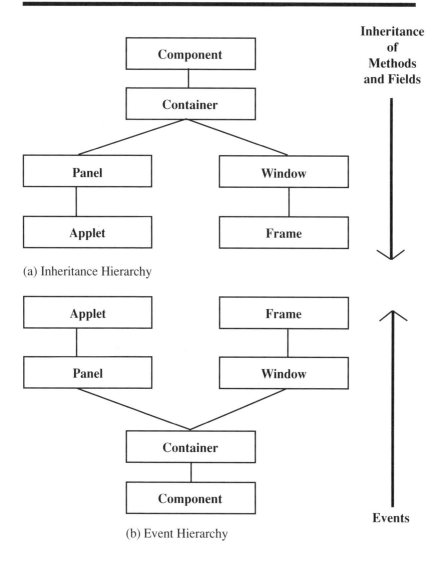

(a) Inheritance Hierarchy

(b) Event Hierarchy

Figure 6.2 Component Hierarchy

4. Change the name of the applet, which is displayed by the Web browser, to the title of the frame. The `setTitle()` method can be used for this purpose.

5. Rename the source file if necessary. The compiler finds the primary class (the one that contains either the `main()` or the `init()` method) by looking for a class with the same name as the primary source file, minus, of course, the .java extension.

The easy convertibility between applets and frames is a well-conceived aspect of Java design.

Use of Java Applets in Networking

Since networking is so important for Applets, many of the concepts that a Java programmer must master—URLs, Hypertext Markup Language (HTML), security concerns, etc.—pertain to networking.

A distributed networking system implies a significant degree of interaction between the software on the client and on the server. However, a high degree of interaction can create security problems, particularly when the client can be any computer on the Internet. Java circumnavigates server security concerns by running applets on the client. This is possible because Java is a cross-platform language. Even when an applet runs on a client, it does so only under tightly controlled conditions.

Another important networking concept is that an applet is not in control of its own thread of execution. An applet must quickly respond to events, then return control to the browser so the user can make a request at any time. An applet that performs a time-consuming task, such as animation, must create a separate thread that it *does* have control of. An example of an applet creating a separate thread will be presented in Section 6.2.2.

6.1 Hypertext Markup Language (HTML)

Hypertext Markup Language is based strictly on ASCII so all that is needed to create an HTML document is a text editor or word processor. However, ASCII text formatting such as tabs, page breaks, and multiple spaces are all considered to be a single space. This means that the creator of HTML files must know how to define the document structure using HTML tags such as <P>, which indicates a new paragraph.

The details of HTML are beyond the scope of this book, but the basics of how to create an HTML document that allows a Web browser or applet viewer to run an applet will be covered later.

6.1.1 Use of URLs in Accessing HTML Documents

Browsers navigate the Web using URLs as descriptors of how to locate and access the next link or Internet resource. URLs were covered in more detail in Chapter 5, but the following is an example of a URL and a description of its three main parts:

```
http://nethost.com/doc_dir/app_info.html
```

1. **Scheme**: The first part of the URL specifies the protocol to be used to access the resource. In the above example, the URL specifies that the Hypertext Transport Protocol (HTTP) should be used to transfer the resource. The scheme is separated from the rest of the resource by a colon and two slashes.

2. **Host Name**: The domain name of the host system that contains the resource. For this example, the host name is nethost.com.

3. **File Name**: The directory or file that contains the resource. If just a directory name, but no file name is supplied, the URL will end in a slash. In this example, the file name, app_info.html, is directly supplied by the URL.

The resource accessed by the URL we have just described, app_info.html, is a Hypertext Markup Language document. This is indicated by the .html extension. Once the HTML document has been loaded by a Java-enabled browser, its contents would be displayed as a Web page, and if it contained an <Applet> tag the applet would be loaded and executed. Figure 6.3 depicts the resource transfer cycle between the browser (client) and the server.

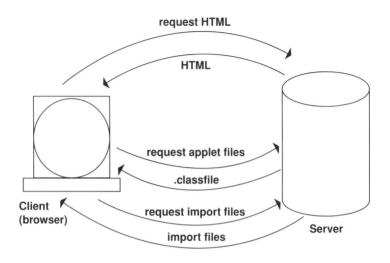

Figure 6.3 Resource Transfer Cycle

6.1.2 Applets and HTML Tags

Most HTML tags consist of a beginning tag and an ending tag. For example, the beginning tag of an HTML document is <HTML>, and the ending tag is </HTML>. The enclosed alphabetic characters are referred to as elements. The element of the <Applet> and </Applet> tags is Applet and the element of the <p> tag is p. Elements are case insensitive, but it is good practice for the document creator to stick with a consistent pattern of uppercase, lowercase, or mixed-case elements.

The HTML document shown in Sample Program 6.4 would contain sufficient information to allow a Java-enabled Web browser to display an applet.

Sample Program 6.4

```
<HTML>
<HEAD>
<TITLE> XYZ Company Home Page </TITLE>
<CENTER>
```

```
<H3> A Java Programmed Site </H3>
<HR>
</HEAD>
<BODY>
<APPLET CODE="xyzco" WIDTH=400 HEIGHT=350>
<PARAM NAME=width VALUE="390">
<PARAM NAME=height VALUE="300">
</APPLET>
</CENTER>
</BODY>
</HTML>
```

An HTML document is basically made up of two parts: a HEAD and a BODY. The HEAD may contain a TITLE, other lines of text of various sizes, and ruled lines. The size of the text in the HEAD may be varied by inserting the <H1> through <H6> tags (the lower the number, the larger the font), and ruled lines can be added by inserting the <HR> tag. The <CENTER> tag causes the text following it to be centered on the Web page.

The place to look for <APPLET> tags is in the body of the HTML document. The beginning <APPLET> tag includes attributes (see Sample Program 6.4) that provide the browser with information regarding how to load and run the applet. Three of these attributes are required:

1. the CODE attribute which is assigned the name of the applet file (the xyzco.class file would be loaded from the server),

2. the WIDTH attribute (the browser would allow an initial width of 400 for the applet), and

3. the HEIGHT attribute (the browser would allow an initial height of 350). Attributes are case insensitive, but the pattern of the cases used for various attributes should be consistent.

The <PARAM> tag is important because it allows the same applet to have a different look and feel from one Web page to another. Although this is one of the few tags that does not require an ending tag, the <PARAM> tag does require two attributes: the NAME attribute and the VALUE attribute. The Applet class's `getParameter()` method returns a `String` object that represents the VALUE of a specified parameter. For example, an applet could obtain the width parameter by the following:

```
int width = Integer.parseInt ((getParameter ("width"));
```

The `parseInt()` method of the Integer class converts a string to an integer, so the result of the above statement would be `width` assigned a value of 300 (see Sample Program 6.4). Note that the values specified by the <PARAM> tags are less than the respective HEIGHT and WIDTH attributes assigned in the beginning <APPLET> tag. This would mean that the initial size of the applet window on the Web page would be somewhat less than the room that would be allocated by the browser. An applet may size itself internally by using literals—in fact no <PARAM> tags at all are required. On the other hand, there is no upper limit to the number of <PARAM> tags. Because <PARAM> attributes are assigned string values, they are easily convertible to any primitive data type. This makes it convenient to use <PARAM> tags for almost any purpose the programmer and HTML document creator consider to be useful.

The <APPLET> and <PARAM> tags are Java extensions to HTML. In other words, they were officially added to HTML Version 3.2 specifically for the purpose of running applets. Sample Program 6.5 shows the formal syntax for the HTML <APPLET> tag—the optional attributes are italicized.

Sample Program 6.5 <APPLET> Syntax

```
<APPLET
  CODE = Applet_Filename
  WIDTH = Integer_Pixel_Width
  HEIGHT = Integer_Pixel_Height
  OBJECT = Serialized_Applet_File_Name
  ARCHIVE = Jar_File_List
  CODEBASE = Url_Base
  ALT = Alternate_Text_Display
  NAME = Applet_Name
  ALIGN = Applet_Window_Alignment
  VSPACE = Vertical_White_Space
  HSPACE = Horizontal_White_Space
>
<PARAM NAME = Parameter_1 VALUE = Value_1>
<PARAM NAME = Parameter_2 VALUE = Value_2>
  . . .
```

```
<PARAM NAME = Parameter_N VALUE = Value_N>
[Alternate HTML Content for non-Java-enabled Web browsers]
</APPLET>
```

The creator of the HTML document should always allow for non-Java-enabled browsers, as shown in the second to last line of Sample Program 6.5. This could be HTML tags that prompt the browser to display an image and a text explanation. The image could be a GIF file of the initial applet, and the text could explain what options would have been available.

A Web browser that is not Java-enabled but is able to recognize <APPLET> tags will ignore the attributes enclosed in the <APPLET> and <PARAM> tags. It will process and display all other HTML information between the opening and ending <APPLET> tags. A Java-enabled browser will only process attributes enclosed in the <APPLET> and <PARAM> tags, ignoring everything else prior to the ending </APPLET> tag. The only exception is HTML comments which are disregarded by all browsers. Comments are set off in the following way:

```
<!- text comment ->
```

There are three required and eight optional <APPLET> attributes shown in Sample Program 6.5. Their significance can be described as follows:

1. **CODE**: Defines the name of the compiled class file that extends `java.applet.Applet`.

2. **WIDTH**: The horizontal width in pixels that the applet occupies on the Web page.

3. **HEIGHT**: The vertical width in pixels that the applet occupies on the Web page.

4. *OBJECT*: This attribute specifies the file name of an applet whose `init()` method is presumed to have been already called, so only its `start()` is invoked. If an applet is specified in this way, it is referred to as a serialized applet.

5. *ARCHIVE*: Contains the list of files contained in a Java ARchive (JAR) file. A JAR file is a compressed ZIP file that may contain multiple files. An applet may require numerous files to be executed for two reasons: (1) The Java compiler creates a separate

file for each public class, and (2) the applet may, in addition, utilize audio and image files. If the browser has to establish a URL connection for each file, substantial additional overhead is involved. A JAR file allows a browser to load all of an applet's files with a single URL connection. This attribute does not, however, replace the need for the CODE attribute.

6. *CODEBASE*: The URL base of the applet's primary file. This attribute is used when the applet's files are not stored in the same directory as the original HTML document. The directory specified may be on the same server, or a different server, as the HTML document. The CODEBASE allows the browser to locate an applet, if it is at a different location, without changing the URL displayed by the browser. The CODEBASE URL is used to specify a directory only, and as such, should end in a slash.

7. *ALT*: This optional attribute is made available to allow for browsers that recognize applet tags, but are not Java enabled. The ALT is assigned to a text string that is displayed an alternative to a blank space on the Web page. Instead of this option, alternate HTML content could be included outside the <APPLET> or <PARAM> tags (see Sample Program 6.5).

8. *NAME*: This attribute, if used, allows a name to be assigned to an applet instance. If more than one applet is running, they may look up each other by name and communicate.

9. *ALIGN*: Specifies the applets alignment on the Web page. For example, ALIGN=RIGHT causes the applet to be aligned with the right side of the browser. Other ALIGN values are: CENTER, LEFT, TOP, TEXTTOP, MIDDLE, ABSMIDDLE, BASELINE, BOTTOM, and ABSBOTTOM.

10. *VSPACE*: Allows the HTML document to define the amount of whitespace, in pixels, above and below the applet.

11. *HSPACE*: Allows the HTML document to define the amount of whitespace, in pixels, to the left and right of the applet.

6.2 Building Applets for the Web

The way to design an applet is to draw, on quadrille paper, a simplified representation of each view-screen of the possible applet states. That may sound a little tedious, but if the components and images are represented by rectangles—with the details left out—the first part of the design phase can be accomplished quickly. This technique has an added bonus in that the coordinates are easily transferable from the quadrille paper to the applet code.

The next step is to make a list of the required components, then a list of the methods and variables needed to manipulate those components. Then the methods, variables, and components can be organized into a high level class structure. The last step is the coding of the details of the variables, methods, and object declarations. One of the advantages of object-oriented programming is that if the programmer realizes that an object has been left out during the design phase, it can easily be added during the coding phase.

One of the things that should be determined during the design phase is the parameters to be obtained from the HTML document. As stated earlier, <PARAM> tags allow the same applet to have a different look and feel, or even perform different functions. But the programmer may not necessarily want the applet's look and feel, or what it does, to vary that much. Furthermore, excessive HTML parameters complicate both the applet code and the HTML document, so <PARAM> tags should be kept to a minimum, except when there are compelling reasons to use them.

6.2.1 An Applet That Traverses the Web

The default layout for applets is the `flowLayout()`—the same layout as its superclass, the Panel class. However, any of the layouts available to the container class, such as the `gridBagLayout()`, are also available to applets. This is because an applet is also a container, inheriting container capabilities. Also, the `move()` method can be used to relocate components, as we will show in the next example.

Applets are frequently used to display images and to play sound clips. Images can be obtained using the getImage() method, and displayed using the showImage() method. Sound clips are obtained by means of the getClip() method and played using the play() method.

An applet can be used to provide a highly descriptive display which will allow the user to log onto another Web site. To do this, the Applet class provides:

1. the getContext() method which obtains a reference to the context (the browser)

2. the showStatus() method which will display a string on the browser's status bar, and

3. the showDocument() method which will cause the browser to display an HTML document from another Web site. An applet that does this is presented in Sample Program 6.6.

Sample Program 6.6 Web Applet

```
// WebApp.java
//
import java.awt.*;
import java.applet.*;
import java.net.*;
public class WebApp extends Applet {

        /* Declare two buttons, an image object that will
           later hold a GIF image of the logos of Sun
           Microsystems and Borland International, and an
           URL object to access the GIF and sound clip. */

     Button sunButton; // Sun Microsystems Button
     Button borButton; // Borland International Button
     Image logoImg;     // Declare Image object
     URL baseUrl;       // Declare URL object

       /* These objects will hold the parameters obtained
          from the HTML document. */
```

```java
Color back, fore;     // Foreground & background colors
int width, height;    // Dimensions of applet
String sb, sf;        // String colors
String sw, sh;        // String dimensions

    /* This object will hold the graphics context used
       to paint the buttons and image of the applet. */

Graphics graphics;  // Declare Graphics Context

    // This boolean allows the buttons to be tried twice.

boolean triedOnce = false;
public void init () {

    /* Create instances of two buttons and add them as
       if it was a flowlayout - they will later be moved.*/

    sunButton = new Button ("Sun");
    borButton = new Button ("Borland");
    add (sunButton);  // Add button to applet
    add (borButton);  // Add button to applet

    // Get all the parameters from the HTML document.

    sf = getParameter ("fore");
    sb = getParameter ("back");
    sw = getParameter ("width");
    sh = getParameter ("height");

    /* Check if parameters are valid (non-null), if they
       are set foreground and background colors and size
       of the applet, else rely on default values. */

if (sf != null) {
   fore = new Color (Integer.parseInt (sf, 16));
   setForeground (fore);
}
else if (sf == null) setForeground (Color.cyan);
```

```java
if (sb != null) {
   back = new Color (Integer.parseInt (sb, 16));
   setBackground (back);
}
else if (sf == null) setBackground (Color.blue);

if (sw != null) width = Integer.parseInt (sw);
else if (sw == null) width = 390;

if (sh != null) height = Integer.parseInt (sh);
else if (sh == null) height = 300;

resize (width, height);  // Set size of applet

/* Get the code base from the HTML, then use that
   URL to load the GIF of the logos of Sun and
   Borland using an Image object to hold it. */

baseUrl = getCodeBase ();        // CODEBASE in HTML
logoImg = getImage (baseUrl, "logos.gif");

paint (graphics);                // Paint applet
play (baseUrl, "bgaudio.au");   // Play audio clip
}

/* This method overrides component's paint method
   in order to paint the applet. */

public void paint (Graphics g) {
   sunButton.resize (70, 40);
   borButton.resize (70, 40);
   sunButton.move (240, 20);     // Relocate button
   borButton.move (240, 80);     // Relocate button

   // Draw the image of the two logos

   g.drawImage (logoImg, 20, 60, this);
}
```

```
// Override Component class's action() method

public boolean action (Event evt, Object arg) {
    AppletContext browser;    // Holds browser reference
    String strUrl = null;     // URL in string form
    URL url;                  // URL of next Web site

    // If true, Sun Web site URL assigned to string

    if (arg == "Sun")
    strUrl = "http://www.sun.com";

    // If true, Borland Web site URL assigned to string

    if (arg == "Borland")
    strUrl = "http://www.borland.com";
    try {

        /* Convert string to URL object, get the browser
           reference, then log onto next Web site. */

        if (strUrl != null) {
            url = new URL (strUrl);
            browser = getAppletContext ();
            browser.showDocument (url);
        }
    }
    catch (MalformedURLException e) {
        if (triedOnce == true ) destroy ();
        else triedOnce = true;
    }
    return true;
}
public void destroy () {
    logoImg.flush (); // Free image memory
    System.exit (1);  // Result in applet being unloaded
}
}
```

In the above applet, four parameters are obtained from an HTML document: width, height, foreground color, and background color. It is desirable for the dimensions of the applet's initial view-screen to be consistent with HTML parameters, because the browser will not display a larger applet than what it finds in the <APPLET> tag. However, if the applet displays additional windows, they are not constrained by the initial width and height. The HTML document is shown below in Sample Program 6.7. The second to last line is a <SRC> tag which causes an alternative image to be displayed for non-Java-enabled browsers. Note: The color parameters are entered in hex, as opposed to decimal.

Sample Program 6.7 HTML Document for Web Applet

```
<HTML>
<HEAD>
<TITLE> Software Company Gateway </TITLE>
<CENTER>
<H3> Select Web site and click on button </H3>
<HR>
</HEAD>
<BODY>
<APPLET CODE="WebApp" WIDTH=400 HEIGHT=350
 CODEBASE="http://nethost.com/java/img_snd/">
<PARAM NAME=width VALUE="400">
<PARAM NAME=height VALUE="350">
<PARAM NAME=foreground VALUE="0000FF">
<PARAM NAME=background VALUE="FFCCCC">
</APPLET>
<SRC logoimg.GIF>
</CENTER>
</BODY>
</HTML>
```

6.2.2 An Animation Applet

A popular use of applets is animation. The source of most of the animation on the Web is a program named Animator, which is provided by the Java Development Kit (JDK). We will create our own animation program.

A basic animation program, GifAnimator, is shown in Sample Program 6.8. GifAnimator retrieves a numbered series of GIF files from a Web location, and proceeds to displays them in rapid succession.

A few of Java's idiosyncrasies appear in this program; they should be understood before studying the program. The first of these regards how an instance of the Vector class is used to store and retrieve GIF images. Vector, included in the `java.util` package, is provided to store objects—an object is either an instance of a class, or an array. But Vector considers all of its elements to be instances of the Object superclass. So when an image is retrieved from the Vector, `images` (in the `paint()` method), it must be recast as an `Image` object. Also, the Integer class, included in the `java.lang` package, can be used to not only store a number in integer form, but also its `String` representation. Regardless of how it was stored, the integer can be retrieved as an `int`. Another new and slightly confusing concept is that an `update()` method is defined, but there are no calls to `update()` anywhere in the code, and also it is not clear where its parameter, `g`, came from. What happens is that when the `repaint()` method is called, the `AWT` automatically invokes `update()`, with the `AWT` providing its parameter. The parameter `AWT` provided for `update()` is either the Graphics context of the current component—if one exists—or a newly created Graphics context with default values. One other note: The `getDocumentBase()` method, a member of the Applet class, retrieves the location of the HTML file which causes the applet to be run.

Sample Program 6.8 GIFAnimator Applet

```
// GifAnimator.java
//
import java.util.*;
import java.awt.*;
import java.applet.*;
import java.net.*;

public class GifAnimator extends Applet implements Runnable {

    Vector images;     // An instance of the Vector class is
                       // expandable array of objects.
```

```
URL docUrl;         // URL of the document base
Integer integer;    // Integer class has useful methods
int imgNbr, currentImage = 1;
Thread appThread;   // Thread will provide animation
Image img;          // Declare Image object
```

/* The init() method first creates an expandable array
   to hold the GIFs, images, then retrieves the number of
   images from the HTML document - storing them as a
   String in integer, next it utilizes integer.intValue()
   to retrieve the int value, then it gets the base URL
   of the GIF file location, and finally retrieves the
   GIF files - storing them as objects in the Vector,
   images.*/

```
public void init () {
   images = new Vector ();
   integer = new Integer (getParameter("imgNumber"));
   imgNbr = integer.intValue ();
   docUrl = getDocumentBase ();
   for (int x = 0; x < imgNbr; x++) {
      img = getImage(docUrl, "imgdir/img" + (x + 1));
      images.addElement(img);
   }
}
public void paint (Graphics g) {
```

/* First, paint() utilizes the Vector class's
   elementAt() method to return the current image object
   - recasting it as a true Image object.*/

```
      img = (Image)images.elementAt(currentImage++);
```

/* Next, it draws the image, with initial x & y
   coordinates equal to zero, and the ImageObserver set
   to null. */

```
   g.drawImage (img, 0, 0, null); // Draw GIF image
   currentImage %= imgNbr;
}
```

```
public void update (Graphics g) {
  paint (g); // Update by painting new image
}
public void start () {
  appThread = new Thread (this); // Create thread
  appThread.start ();            // so can return
                                 // control to browser
}
public void run () {
  while (true) {
    repaint (); // Calls update(), supplying it
                // with a Graphics object, g.
    try { appThread.sleep (100); }
    catch (InterruptedException e) {}
  }
}
public void stop () {    // Stop method of applet
    appThread.stop (); // Stop method of thread
}
}
```

An HTML document that would work with GifAnimator is shown below:

Sample Program 6.9 HTML Document for GifAnimator

```
<HTML>
<BODY>
<APPLET CODE="GifAnimator.class" HEIGHT=240 WIDTH=340>
<PARAM NAME="imgNbr" VALUE="7">
</APPLET>
</BODY>
</HTML>
```

6.2.3 Animation Flicker

If GifAnimator was run the way it is listed in Sample Program 6.9, there would be, in all likelihood, a problem with flicker. The most common technique used to alleviate flicker is known as *double buffering*. The flicker problem in GifAnimator could be solved by inserting a total of five statements and one method. First, two additional declarations should be added to the declaration section, just prior to `init()`:

```
Image offScreenImage;          // Off-screen drawing surface
Graphics offScreenGraphics     // Off-screen Graphics context
```

The next step would be to add two statements that create instances of the Image and Graphics classes. These could go anywhere in the `init()` method:

```
/* size() is a component method that returns a simple
   Dimension object, whose width and size fields contain
   the component's dimensions - size() is utilized by
   createImage() to create an off-screen drawing surface
   (an Image object) the same size as the applet.*/

offScreenImage = createImage (size().width, size().height);

/* Both the Component and Image classes include a
   getGraphics() method, and both return a new Graphics
   context object. This one is a Graphics method.*/

 offScreenGraphics = offScreenImage.getGraphics ();
```

The third step would be to add the method `flickerFix()` to the GifAnimator class. This method (below) sets the color of the off-screen Graphics context to the background color of the component, clears the off-screen image utilizing the `fillRect()` method, then resets the off-screen Graphics context color to the foreground color of the component. Next, `flickerFix()` draws the off-screen image. Note: Even though the first four statements were only qualified by `offScreenGraphics`, `offScreenImage` contains the `Image` object, because `offScreenGraphics` was created from `offScreenImage`.

```
private Image flickerFix (Image img) {
   offScreenGraphics.setColor (getBackGround());
   offScreenGraphics.fillRect (0, 0, size().width,
         size().height);
   offScreenGraphics.setColor (getForeGround());
   offScreenGraphics.drawImage (img, 0, 0, null);
```

```
   return offScreenImage;
}
```

The last step would be to add one statement to the paint() method – just before the g.drawImage() method is called:

```
img = flickerFix (img);
```

The above code appears to be doing the same thing as before: drawing an Image object to an on-screen drawing surface. But, there is an important difference. Once an image has been drawn off-screen, it is in a different format. It can then be transferred to the screen so rapidly that it is imperceptible to the eye.

The first two statements in the flickerFix() method—the ones that cleared the off-screen drawing surface—are not really necessary for GifAnimator. That is because GifAnimator displays images that are exactly the same size as the container. However, for animation that draws smaller images, or that scrolls text, it is useful to clear the whole display area, then draw the image. In fact, one of the problems with overriding the update() method is that the paint() method usually expects update() to clear the background. Thus, great care should be taken when overriding either of these two Component class methods.

There are strategies, other than an off-screen clearing and redrawing, that are employed to reduce flicker. One involves using the clipRect() and clearRect() methods to clear only the area that is going to be redrawn—with this followed by drawing the new image at a slightly different location. This technique can be used in conjunction with double buffering, to produce faster animation, and to reduce animation flicker still further.

CHAPTER 7

Java Applications

Applets are usually loaded from remote hosts, while applications are executed on the local host. Aside from this obvious difference, users have different expectations of an application. For example, an applet is not expected to include a menu bar or a dialog box, because these functions are usually handled by the browser. Also, applications are larger and may include many windows.

The biggest advantage of writing a program in Java, whether it is an applet or an application, is that Java is a cross-platform language—meaning a program only has to be designed, coded, and debugged once. However, Java applications have been hampered because the Java interpreter (which isn't readily available on every system) must be loaded every time a Java program is run. This is due to change. MicroSoft, IBM, and Apple are including the Java virtual machine as part of their new operating systems. Also, Sun Microsystems has developed an all-Java operating system called Kona.

Advantages of Java Applications vs. Applets

The first advantage an application has over an applet is performance. Because an application does not have the overhead of the browser and because the amount of accessible memory is not restricted, applications run slightly faster. Secondly, applications are not restricted by the "sandbox". An applet can not write or read to local files. Also, an applet may only establish a URL connection to the hosts from which the class files and/or the HTML document was downloaded. On the other hand, an application may write and read to numerous local files and may establish a URL connection to any host it pleases—including anywhere on the Internet.

In this chapter, an application that combines the concept of a GUI with the concept of multiple threads communicating by means of pipe streams will be developed. The basics of the `main()` method, which is required for all applications, and the classes added to Java 1.1 for event processing will also be discussed. The new `Event` classes will later be used to build the example application at the end of the chapter.

7.1 Source Filenames, The Main Method, and Invoking the Compiler and Interpreter

A Java source file can contain more than one class definition, but at most one public class. Source filenames must be the same as the name of the first class defined in each file, plus the `.java` extension. If a source file contains a public class it is required to be the first class in the file. Since Java is case sensitive, a source file must be named using the same case as the source file's first class (even if the operating system is not case sensitive).

The primary file of a Java application is the file that contains the `main()` method. The first class contained in the primary file is the one that includes the `main()` method. This class is referred to as the primary class, it is nearly always declared public, and it must have the same name as the primary file. For example, if the `main()` method is defined in a class named `PrimaryClass`, the primary file would be named `PrimaryClass.java`. The appropriate commands to compile and run this application would be:

```
javac PrimaryClass
java PrimaryClass
```

The `javac` and `java` commands are used to invoke the Java compiler and interpreter, respectively. The Java compiler creates a separate bytecode file for each application class. The compiler gives each bytecode file the same name as the class it was compiled from, except that it adds a

.class extension. Since there are usually many .class files, it is advisable to create a separate directory for each application. If the Java Development Kit (JDK) has been installed correctly, the operating system is able to execute the Java compiler and interpreter from within the application program's directory.

The Main Method

The prototype of the main() method must have the following following form:

```
public static void main (String args [])
```

The access modifier for the main() method is declared public, so that it is accessible from other programs. The static modifier is declared so the main() method cannot be overridden by a subclass. The return type is void, because Java programs, unlike C/C++, have no return value. However, the System.exit() method can be used to return a parameter to the operating system. The main() method has a single parameter args, an array of String objects. The variable name args is chosen by convention, and the array it represents is used to hold the arguments entered by the user on the command line.

The following brief program includes an example of a main() method:

```
class MainClass {
  long longInt = 100;
  public static void main (String args []) {
    long local;
    MainClass m;
    m = new MainClass ();
    local = m.longInt;
    System.out.println ("Long Integer = " + local);
  }
}
```

The main() method is invoked by the interpreter when the program is started. On the third line of the main() method an object of MainClass, m, is created. It would seem, at first, that there would be no reason for MainClass to be instantiated within the main() method, because normally methods can access all fields and methods within their own class. But, since the main() method is declared static, there is only one copy of it in memory—which is immediately loaded by the Java virtual machine. And since the rest of MainClass does not exist until it has been instantiated, the main() method has no reference to it. It is for this reason that main() created a reference to MainClass—by instantiating the object m—on the third line.

When execution begins, the Java interpreter invokes the main() method. The interpreter then runs until the main() method returns, or until it reaches the end of main(). If one or more threads are still running, the interpreter continues until all threads terminate. If the interpreter encounters a System.exit(), the execution of all threads is discontinued, and the interpreter exits.

7.2 Processing Application Program Events

It was by design, rather than by accident, that the java.awt.event package and the capability of defining local inner classes were both added with the release of Java version 1.1. In this section the details of how events are recognized and how local classes can be used to process Java 1.1 events will be discussed.

7.2.1 More on Java 1.1 Event Processing

As was shown in Table 5.3 in Chapter 5, a KeyEvent can be generated by any component. If one of the KeyEventListener methods is invoked, the Boolean isAction() method can be utilized to determine if key was a keyboard control key. If isAction() returns true, getKeyCode() can be compared to the following KeyEvent constants:

KeyEvent.LEFT	KeyEvent.PRINT_SCREEN
KeyEvent.RIGHT	KeyEvent.SCROLL_LOCK
KeyEvent.UP	KeyEvent.CAPS_LOCK
KeyEvent.DOWN	KeyEvent.NUM_LOCK
KeyEvent.END	KeyEvent.PAUSE
KeyEvent.PGDN	KeyEvent.INSERT
KeyEvent.PGUP	KeyEvent.DELETE

KeyEvent.F1-F12   KeyEvent.BACK_SPACE

If the key that was pressed, released, or typed was not a keyboard control key, its ASCII value can be obtained by the getKeyChar() method of the KeyEvent class.

Modifier Keys

Although the TextEvent class includes mask constants and a getModifier() method, it is more straight forward to use the Boolean methods provided:

```java
public boolean isShiftDown ();
public boolean isControlDown ();
public boolean isMetaDown ();
public boolean isAltDown ();
```

Processing 1.1 Events Without Defining Listeners

Event masks are defined in the AWTEvent class that allows the enabling of specific events without defining listeners for them. For example, key events and action events (e.g., enter key) that are caused by typing in a text area can both be enabled and processed by the following code:

```java
class CustomTextArea extends TextArea {
  // Definitions of constant, instance, and static
                    fields
    public CustomTextArea (...) {  // Constructor
      enableEvents (AWTEvent.ACTION_EVENT_MASK |
                  AWTEvent.KEY_EVENT_MASK);
                            // Rest of code for
                            // constructor goes
                            // here.
  }
      . . .
  processKeyEvent (KeyEvent e) {
      // Code to process key event
          super.ProcessKeyEvent (e);
  }
  processActionEvent (ActionEvent e) {
      // Code to process action event
          super.ProcessActionEvent (e);
```

```
   }
}
```

7.2.2 Implementing Event Listeners With Local Classes

The advantage to implementing an event listener with a local class is that it allows the code that processes the event to be adjacent to the code that creates the event, rather than in a separately defined non-local class. Even an inner class does work for this purpose as well. Shown below is a generalized method for creating menu items complete with item listeners and code to process their events:

```
MenuItem menuItem (String label, final int cmd) {
  MenuItem item = new MenuItem (label);
  class MenuItemListener implements ActionListener {
    public void actionPerformed (ActionEvent e) {
      menuAction (cmd);
    }
  }
  ActionListener listener = new MenuItemListener ();
  item.addActionListener (listener);
  return item;
}
```

The createButton() method is a generalized method that creates a button. It also utilizes an anonymous local class to create the button listener, including the code to process action events generated by the button. When an anonymous class is used to define a listener, the new keyword is followed by the name of a listener interface or an event adapter, which in turn is followed by a double parentheses, "()". The double parentheses, "()", is then followed by the definition of the body of the anonymous class. The statement ends with the very unusual brace-parenthesis, "})", sequence, as shown below:

```
Button createButton (String label) {
  Button button = new Button ("label");
  button.setForeground (Color.green);
  button.setBackground (Color.blue);
  button.addActionListener (new ActionListener () {
    public void actionPerformed (ActionEvent e)
    { if (e.getSource() instanceof Button) {
```

```
            hide ();
            toBack (); } } });
    return button;
}
```

7.3 An Example Application: Convert

Our example application, Convert, provides the user with a GUI that includes a menu bar at the top of the screen, a text area in the middle, a panel at the bottom, and a popup window that is not initially displayed. The menu bar has one drop down menu, which is labeled "Setup". The panel contains a text field and two buttons. The text field allows the user to enter a file name. If the file name is valid, the contents of the file are converted from lower case to upper case, or from upper case to lower case—depending on the set-up data. The results are then displayed in the text area, with the text area scrolling, if necessary. If the user entered an invalid file name, the message "No such file, try again" appears in the text area. One of the two buttons contained in the panel clears the text field and the other exits the program.

If the user clicks "Setup" on the menu bar, a drop down menu with three choices appears. The three choices include "Clear," to clear the text area, "Setup," to edit the setup data, and "Exit," to exit the program. If the user selects the "Setup" item, a popup window with three radio buttons is activated.

The three radio buttons are labled "Lower to Upper," "Upper to Lower," and "Default". The user may select only one of the three. If the user selects "Default," the file to be processed will be named "file.def", and the conversion will be from lower to upper case. The popup window also includes an "OK" button, to be clicked when the user is finished with the setup.

The Convert application program consists of four classes:

1. The primary class: Convert. This class performs two primary functions:

    a. The main method creates a graphical user interface object, GUI, by instantiating GraphicalUserInterface.

b. Provides a public method, setUpIO(), that sets up:

    i. An I/O stream that accesses a text file.

    ii. A separate thread of execution.

    iii. A pipe stream between the separate thread and the GUI.

2. A java.lang.Thread subclass: ConCurrent. This class performs three functions:

    a. Accepts, as a constructor parameter, an I/O stream that has been set up to access a text file. The constructor is invoked by setUpIO().

    b. Reads the text file, converting the text to either upper or lower case, depending on the value of a boolean parameter: toUpper.

    c. Sends the converted text file to the GUI through a pipe stream. The pipe stream is first set up by setUpIO().

3. A class that implements the ActionEventListener interface, and that is also a Frame subclass: GraphicalUserInterface. This class performs three functions:

    a. Constructs the GUI which consists of these subcomponents:

        i. A menu bar that offers only one menu, which is labeled "Setup". The setup menu consists of three items: "Clear," to clear the text area, "Setup," to cause a popup window to appear, and "Exit," to terminate the program.

        ii. A text area that displays the contents of the text files after they have been converted to upper or lower case.

        iii. A panel which contains: a "Clear" button, to clear the text field, a "Quit" button, to exit the program, and a text field labeled "Enter file name," to enter the name of a text file.

    b. Provides an actionPerformed() method to process action events not generated by menu items or the popup window. This method processes button events, and the type of event generated by pressing enter when the the text field has been activated.

c. Utilizes a local class to provide a listener for menu item events. The menu items (complete with listener) are created by `createMenu()`.

4. A Window subclass: `Popup`. This class performs these two functions:

a. Utilizes an anonymous class to provide a listener for check box events. The check box items (complete with listener) are created by `checkItem()`. Since the check box items are part of a check box group, they look and act as radio buttons (the user is allowed to select only one).

b. Once instantiated, it provides a popup window that allows the user to edit the set-up data. The window provided by the `Popup` class is modal, i.e., when it is visible, it is the only component that will respond to user input. (Windows are made visible or invisible by invoking the `show()` or `hide()` methods.) The set-up data is stored in the `int` variable `checkBox`. There are three possible values for `checkBox`:

i. lower to upper case conversion of the text contained in the file whose name was entered by the user

ii. upper to lower case conversion of the text contained in the file whose name was entered by user

iii. lower to upper case conversion of the default file ("`file.def`")

As can be seen in Sample Program 7.1 (below), the `main()` method passes an instance of its own class to the constructor of the `GraphicalUserInterface` class. This allows two-way communication between the object responsible for the GUI and the methods of the primary class (the parent of the GUI).

One additional remark: In the `displayPipedText()` method of the `GraphicalUserInterface` class there is a loop that reads one line at a time. The fact that the loop will block on the read helps synchronize the communication between threads, and between methods of different classes. This is because no data is going to be lost since one thread or method is looping faster than another. They just block on the read—or even on the write, if the Java buffers are full—giving a loop in another thread or method time to catch up.

The following is the complete listing for the Convert application program.

Sample Program 7.1 An Example Application Program: Convert

```java
import java.io.*;
import java.awt.*;
import java.awt.event.*;

/* Convert, which is the primary class, provides the
   methods necessary to setup the I/O streams,
   including a pipestream. The pipestream allows a
   separately executing thread, c_thrd, to communicate
   with the main thread. Execution of the separate
   thread is initiated by setUpThread(), also a member
   of the Convert class. */

public class Convert {
  ConCurrent c_thrd;          // Separately executing thread
  GraphicalUserInterface GUI; // Handles all user input

  /* This method creates a DataInputStream, textline,
     that allows a file to be read one line at a time. It
     also fits a PrintStream into a pipe stream, allowing
     text to be piped out one line at a time. The output
     pipe and the stream that accesses the file,
     textline, are handed to a separately executing
     thread by invoking setupThread(). The input pipe is
     returned to the calling method. */

  PipedReader setupIO ( String fileName, boolean
                               toUpper ) {
    try {
      FileReader text_in =
        new FileReader (fileName);
```

```
      BufferedReader textline =
        new BufferedReader (text_in);
      PipedWriter pipeOut =
        new PipedWriter ();
      PipedReader pipeIn =
        new PipedReader (pipeOut);
      PrintWriter printPipe =
        new PrintWriter (pipeOut);
      setupThread (textline, printPipe, toUpper);
      return pipeIn;
    }
    catch (FileNotFoundException e) {}
    catch (IOException e) { System.exit (1); }
    return null;
  }

  /* setupThread() instantiates c_thrd, handing it a
     stream that accesses a file, textline, and a pipe
     back to the main thread, printPipe. Then c_thrd is
     started as a separately executing thread. */

  void setupThread ( BufferedReader textline,
              PrintWriter printPipe, boolean toUpper )
  {
    c_thrd = new ConCurrent (textline, printPipe, toUpper);
    c_thrd.start ();
  }

  /* The main() method first creates an instance of its
     own class, so it will have a reference to it, then
     passes that reference to the constructor of the GUI,
     so it  will have access to its parent's methods.
     Then, the GUI is activated, and allowed to control
     the main thread of execution. */
  public static void main (String args []) {
    Convert convert = new Convert ();
    convert.GUI = new GraphicalUserInterface (convert);
    convert.GUI.setSize (600, 390);
    convert.GUI.show ();                // Activate GUI

}

}
```

/* The ConCurrent class provides a separate thread of execution. Its run() method reads data from a file, processes it, and pipes it back to the main thread (the GUI) for display. ConCurrent relies on the methods of its parent class, Convert, to set up the I/O streams. */

```java
class ConCurrent extends Thread {
  boolean toUpper;          // Convert to upper case
  BufferedReader textline; // Accesses a text file
  PrintWriter printPipe;   // Pipe out a line at a time
```

/* The constructor assigns its own instance fields to the I/O streams and the boolean variable, which are passed to it as parameters. */

```java
  ConCurrent (BufferedReader textline,
            PrintWriter printPipe, boolean toUpper) {
    this.toUpper = toUpper; this.textline = textline;
    this.printPipe = printPipe;
  }
```

/* The thread's run() method reads the data one line at a time, converts it to upper or lower case, and pipes it back to the main thread, the GUI, for display. */

```java
  public void run () {
    try {
      sleep(400);
      String str = dis.readLine ();
      while (str != null) {
```

/* If toUpper = true, the String class method toUpperCase() is invoked, else toLowerCase() is invoked. */

```java
        if (toUpper) str = str.toUpperCase ();
        else str = str.toLowerCase ();
        printPipe.println (str);
        str = textline.readLine ();
      }
      printPipe.flush (); // Output remaining data
    }
```

```
   catch (IOException e) {}
   catch (InterruptedException e) {}
 }
}
```

/* The GraphicalUserInterface class provides the
methods that allow the user to interact with the
program. The only exceptions are the methods of the
Popup class, which provide a popup window and enable
the user to edit the setup. But even in this case,
the popup window is instantiated, and made visible
and invisible by methods of this class. */

```
class GraphicalUserInterface extends Frame
                         implements ActionListener {
   Convert convert;    // Reference to parent's methods
   Popup pw;           // Pop up window
   Panel pnl;          // Contains 2 buttons & textfield
   TextField tf;       // Used to enter file name
   TextArea ta;        // Displays processed text
   Button button;      // Used to create two buttons
   String fn;          // File name entered by user
   MenuBar mb;
   Menu men;
```

/* The constructor's primary responsibility is to
create a GUI. These three methods: createMenuBar(),
createPanel(), and createTextArea() are defined in
this class (see below). They return valid arguments
for two methods inherited from the Frame class:
setMenuBar() and add(). */

```
public GraphicalUserInterface (Convert convert) {
   this.convert = convert;    // Reference to parent
   setTitle ("Convert to upper case");
   setMenuBar (createMenuBar ());
   add ("South", createPanel ()); // BorderLayout is def.
   add ("Center", createTextArea ());
   createPopupWindow ();      // Not visible at first
}
```

/* This method uses a loop and menuItem() (defined
below) to add three menu items to a newly

instantiated MenuBar, mb. */

```
private MenuBar createMenuBar () {
  int currentItem;
  String [] str = { "Clear", "Setup", "Exit", };
  mb = new MenuBar ();
  men = new Menu ("Setup");
  for (int i = 0; i < 3; i++)
    men.add (menuItem (str [i], i));
  mb.add (men); return mb;
}
```

/* This method utilizes a local class, MenuItemListener, to create a menu item (complete with listener). When a menu item created here generates an action event, it is processed by the local actionPerformed() method, which invokes menuAction() (defined below). */

```
MenuItem menuItem (String label, final int cmd) {
  MenuItem item = new MenuItem (label);
  class MenuItemListener implements ActionListener {
    public void actionPerformed (ActionEvent e) {
      menuAction (cmd);
    }
  }
  ActionListener listener = new MenuItemListener ();
  item.addActionListener (listener);
  return item;
}
```

/* This method is called by the menu item listeners to process action events generated by menu items. */

```
private void menuAction (int action) {
  final int clear = 0;
  final int setup = 1;
  final int exit = 2;
  switch (action) {
    case clear:ta.setText ("");// Clear text field break.
    case setup:pw.show ();     // Make popup
               pw.toFront ();  // window visible.
    break;
```

```
      case exit: pw.dispose ();
                 System.exit (1);  // User is done
    }
}

  /* This is a specific method that creates a panel with
     two buttons and a text field. The createButton() and
     createTextField() methods are programmer defined
     (see below). They return valid arguments for add().
     */

  private Panel createPanel () {
    pnl = new Panel ();         // Create Panel object
    pnl.add (createButton ("Clear"));
    pnl.add (createButton ("Quit"));
    pnl.add (new Label ("Enter file name"));
    pnl.add (createTextField ());
    return pnl;
  }

  private Button createButton (String label) {
    button = new Button (label);
    button.setForeground (Color.green);
    button.setBackground (Color.black);
    button.addActionListener (this);
    return button;
  }

  private TextField createTextField () {
    tf = new TextField (14);   // Width = 14 characters
    tf.setForeground (Color.cyan);
    tf.setBackground (Color.black);
    tf.addActionListener (this);
    return tf;
  }

  private TextArea createTextArea () {
    ta = new TextArea ();       // Create TextArea object
    ta.setForeground (Color.cyan);
    ta.setBackground (Color.blue);
    return ta;
  }

  /* This method creates a popup window by instantiating
```

the Popup class. It can later be made visible
(popped up) when needed. */

```
private void createPopupWindow () {
  pw = new Popup (this);
  pw.pack ();
  pw.move (100, 200);
}
```

/* This method is invoked when one of the
subcomponents of the panel generates an action
event. If it is a text field event, actionPerformed()
assumes the user has entered a file name, so it calls
displayPipedText() to display the results (see below).
If the event is generated by a button, executeButtonCmd()
is called (also, see below). */

```
public void actionPerformed (ActionEvent e) {
  if (e.getSource() instanceof TextField)
```

/* The argument for displayPipedText(), textPipe(),
not only returns an input pipe, but also starts a
whole chain of events (see comment for textPipe()).
*/

```
      displayPipedText (textPipe ());
    if (e.getSource() instanceof Button)
      executeButtonCmd (); }
```

/* This method outputs an error message if the input
pipe is null, otherwise it feeds the input pipe into
a BufferedReader, so it can be read one line at a
time, then displays in the text area. */

```
private void displayPipedText (PipedReader pipedTxt) {
  if (pipedTxt == null)
    ta.append ("No such file, try again.");
  else {
    BufferedReader br = new BufferedReader (pipedTxt);
    try {
      ta.setText ("");              // Clear text area
```

/* Block on first read, allowing the ConCurrent
object time to access the file. */

```
    String str = dis.readLine ();
    while (str != null) {
        ta.appendText (str + ''); // Append to
        str = dis.readLine();       // text area
    }
    br.close ();                  // Close current file
    }
    catch (IOException e) {}
}
}
```

/* This method uses a switch statement to decide what parameters to pass to setUpIO(). The tasks performed by setUpIO() are: 1. it starts a separate thread to process the file identified by fn, and 2. it creates a pipe stream back to the main thread. The input end of that pipe stream is returned to the method that called textPipe(). */

```
private PipedReader textPipe () {
    final int lwrToUpr = 0;
    final int uprToLwr = 1;
    final int def = 2;
    PipedReader pipe = null;
    switch (pw.currentBox) {
        case lwrToUpr: fn = tf.getText ();
            pipe = convert.setupIO (fn, true);
            break;
        case uprToLwr: fn = tf.getText ();
            pipe = convert.setupIO (fn, false);
            break;
        case def:      fn = "file.def";
            pipe = convert.setupIO (fn, true);
    }
    return pipe;
}
private void executeButtonCmd (ActionEvent e) {
    if (e.getActionCommand() == "Clear")
        tf.setText ("");       // Clear text field to
                               // enter of new file.
        if (e.getActionCommand() == "Quit") {
```

```
        pw.dispose ();
        System.exit (2);     // User is done
    }
  }
}
```

/* The Popup class provides a modal popup window that allows the user to edit the setup data. */

```
class Popup extends Window {
  int currentBox;       // Contains setup data.
  CheckboxGroup group;
  Button ok_button;
  String str [] = { "LowerToUpperCase",
                    "UpperToLowerCase", "DefaultFile",
  };
```

/* The constructor first establishes the modality of the window (see below), then it builds the popup window by setting the layout, the colors, and by adding the components to the window container. */

```
public Popup (GraphicalUserInterface parent) {
  super (parent);    // Call to super makes window modal
                     // if parameter is the parent frame.
  setLayout (new FlowLayout ());
  setForeground (Color.yellow);
  setBackground (Color.black);
  group = new CheckboxGroup ();
```

/* This loop adds checkbox items to the checkbox group. The checkbox items act as radio buttons (the user can only select one). */

```
  for (int i = 0; i < 3; i++)
    add (checkItem (str [i], group, i)); add
  (createButton ("OK"));
}
```

/* This method utilizes a local class, CheckItemListener, to create a checkbox item (complete with listener). When one of the check boxes generates an item event, the itemStateChanged() method will process it. */

```java
Checkbox checkItem (String label, CheckboxGroup cbg,
                                  final int boxNbr) {
  boolean state = false;
  if (boxNbr == 0) state = true;
  Checkbox item = new Checkbox (label, cbg, state);
  class CheckItemListener implements ItemListener {
    public void itemStateChanged (ItemEvent e) {
      currentBox = boxNbr;
    }
  }
  ItemListener listener = new CheckItemListener();
  item.addItemListener (listener);
  return item;
}

/* This method utilizes an anonymous local class to
   create a button (complete with listener). */

Button createButton (String label) {
  Button button = new Button ("Done");
  button.setForeground (Color.green);
  button.setBackground (Color.blue);
  button.addActionListener (new ActionListener () {
    public void actionPerformed (ActionEvent e)
      { if (e.getSource() instanceof Button) {
          hide ();
          toBack (); } }
  });
  return button;
}
}
```

CHAPTER 8

Advanced Topics: Custom Components, Java Beans, and Java Swing

8.1 Custom Components

Unfortunately, the AWT components do not provide all of the necessary functionality for every Java application. There are times when it is desirable for the programmer to create a custom component in order to make an application user-friendly.

For the sake of giving an example that most readers are familiar with, let us assume that our task is to re-program the Windows Explorer utility in Java. One of the graphical components of the Windows Explorer is a little box that contains either a plus or a minus sign. The minus sign indicates that the directory to the right of the box has been *expanded* (its files and subdirectories made visible and added to the tree structure), while a plus sign indicates that the directory has not been expanded. These little boxes provide a good example of a situation where a customized component is potentially very useful. There are three reasons for this:

1. The potential component (the little box) contains state information. In this case, there are two states: expanded (minus sign) and unexpanded (plus sign).

2. The potential component could conceivably fire useful events. The object that managed the directory could receive events (fired by the little box) that indicated a state change. Then, the directory manager could respond by making its files and subdirectories either visible or invisible, depending on whether the new state was expanded or unexpanded.

3. The potential component is graphical, and used in a lot of different places. If a GUI includes a non-standard component, it is helpful if the user interacts with it repeatedly, gaining familiarity.

8.1.1 Design Strategies for Custom Components

Once the decision has been made to create a custom component, the next step is to select the design strategy. There are three basic design strategies:

1. Subclassing of the Component or the Canvas class.

2. Subclassing of specialized AWT component (e.g., text fields, text areas, dialog boxes).

3. Subclassing of the Container class (aggregation strategy).

Subclassing of the Component or the Canvas Class

Both the Component and Canvas classes are very generalized. Except for the menu components, Component is the superclass of all Java components. Canvas is a slightly modified subclass of Component, with only the `paint()` and `addNotify()` methods overridden. Part of the reason the Canvas class was included in the AWT was that programmers could use it to create custom components (the remaining motivation was to provide a drawing surface for GUIs). Component and Canvas do not have their own graphical displays, nor can they include other components, because they are not containers. Components that subclass Component or

Canvas must be drawn from scratch. This is done by overriding the `paint()` method.

This design strategy is often employed to allow the user to input data that cannot be accepted by standard components (e.g., text fields, choice boxes, etc.). An example of this type of input would be a component that allows the user to click the mouse when the cursor is at different points within a Cartesian coordinate system. The component could then draw a graph through these points when, for example, Enter is pressed.

Subclassing of Specialized AWT Components

This strategy of subclassing of specialized AWT components is employed when an already available component provides most of the functionality required. A good example is a customized Textfield that allows the user to enter a password with the keystrokes only echoed with asterisks.

Container Subclassing (Aggregation Strategy)

The aggregation strategy, which involves combining existing components in a Container subclass, is employed when:

1. An application requires two or more components to work closely together.

2. Their combined functionality has a strong potential for reuse.

A good example of an aggregate component would be a popup window that allows students to indicate the foreign language that would be their first preference. A checkbox group could be labeled with four or five of the most requested languages, perhaps French, German, Spanish, and Japanese. A drop-down choice box, which included perhaps Italian and Russian, could offer a second tier of roughly twenty languages. A text field could be used to enter more obscure languages (e.g., if enough students entered Tagalog, a course could be offered). This example would meet the first criteria for an aggregate custom component because the three subcomponents would have to work closely together to prevent more than one selection. As for the second criteria, this component would have a strong potential for reuse if it had accessor methods to set the checkbox labels, choice items, and allowable text field input.

8.1.2 Example of a Custom Component

The design strategy for this example will be Component subclassing. The name of the class that subclasses Component will be DirectoryNode. The function of this component will be to provide an all-purpose node for a disk directory utility program. This program will be similar to Windows Explorer, but will take a simpler approach.

There are three steps necessary to develop a custom component:

1. Develop a custom event class by extending AWTEvent. (It is preferable to follow the xxxEvent naming convention.)

2. Develop a listener interface which can be implemented by potential listeners. (It is preferable to follow the xxxListener naming convention.)

3. Develop a custom component class that includes methods to add and remove listeners, and to fire events:

```
public void addxxxListener (xxxListener l);
public void removexxxListener (xxxListener l);
protected void processxxxEvent (xxxEvent e);
```

Developing a Custom Event Class

A custom event class must include instance variables to hold: (1) the state of the component firing the event, and (2) any identifying information of that component (see nodeName and nodeType below). An event class requires a constructor that accepts as parameters all state and identifying information, plus a reference to the source. The constructor first invokes the AWTEvent superclass to save the source and the event id, then assigns the state and identifying information. Finally, a custom event class must provide accessor methods for potential listeners, as shown below:

```
public class DirectoryNodeEvent extends AWTEvent {
    // Constant definitions will go here
    protected int nodeState;   // State of node firing event
    protected String nodeName; // Name of file or directory
    protected String nodeType;
    // Three types: "File", "Dir", and "Root".
    public DirectoryNodeEvent (DirectoryNode source,
```

```
                 String   nodeType,
                 String   nodeName,
                 int      nodeState)
  {
     super (source, RESERVED_ID_MAX + 1);
  // Code to assign instance variables to parameters
  }

  // Public accessor methods
  public int getNodeState () { return nodeState };
  public String getNodeType () { return nodeType };
  public String getNodeName () { return nodeName };
}
```

Developing a Listener Interface

Custom listener interfaces follow the naming conventions established by the java.awt.event package. A listener interface must define a method prototype for each event type defined by that event. For example, a KeyEvent can be generated in three different ways: (1) key pressed, (2) key released, or (3) key typed. There are three corresponding method prototypes defined by the KeyEventListener: keyPressed(), keyReleased(), and keyTyped(). Our example will have only one event type, which indicates a node state change, and there will be one corresponding method prototype defined by our listener interface: nodeStateChanged(). Following the standard naming convention, our listener interface is named DirectoryNodeEventListener, and is shown below:

```
public interface DirectoryNodeEventListener extends
    java.util.EventListener {
  public void nodeStateChanged (DirectoryNodeEvent e);
}
```

Developing a Custom Component

A custom component consists of a class that must contain methods to add and remove event listeners, plus any helper classes. The DirectoryNode component will be simple enough that no helper classes are needed.

The DirectoryNode component appears as a rectangle with two labels inside. The first label indicates whether the node is a file, a directory, or the root directory. The second label is the name of the file or directory.

The state of the node changes every time the user clicks on the node component. The user is made aware of the node's state by its current foreground and background colors. There are three states: (1) highlighted (magenta background, bright cyan foreground), (2) selected (black background, bright yellow foreground), and (3) released (blue background, bright cyan foreground). The default state is released.

How the DirectoryNode component is used is left to the application programmer. One possible use might be for a selected file node to display its contents (perhaps, to the side of the directory tree). Another possibility would be for a selected directory node to expand, adding its files and subdirectories to the tree.

The complete listing for the directory node component, including its customized event class, customized listener interface, and an applet to test it, is shown below:

Sample Program 8.1
Directory Node Customized Component

```
// DirectoryNode.java

    import java.awt.*;
    import java.awt.event.*;
    import java.util.*;
    import java.applet.Applet;

/* DirectoryNodeEvent is the custom event class for the
DirectoryNode component. It includes public instance
fields and accessor methods for all necessary state
and identifier information. Also included are the
constants required to identify the current node state
and type.*/
    class DirectoryNodeEvent extends AWTEvent {

      // These constants identify the current node state.

        public static final int HIGH_LIGHTED = 1;
        public static final int SELECTED = 2;
        public static final int RELEASED = 3;

      // These constants identify the node type.
```

```java
public static final String DIR = "Dir";
public static final String FILE = "File";
public static final String ROOT = "Root";

protected int nodeState;      // State of node firing
                              // event
protected String nodeName;    // Name of file or
                              // directory
protected String nodeType;    // Three types: "File",
                              // "Dir", and "Root".

public DirectoryNodeEvent (DirectoryNode source,
        String nodeType,
        String nodeName,
        int nodeState)
{
        super (source, RESERVED_ID_MAX + 1);
        this.nodeState = nodeState;
        this.nodeType = nodeType;
        this.nodeName = nodeName;
}

// Public accessor methods

public int getNodeState () { return nodeState ;};
public String getNodeType () { return nodeType ;};
public String getNodeName () { return nodeName ;};
}


    interface DirectoryNodeListener extends
            java.util.EventListener {
        public void nodeStateChanged (DirectoryNodeEvent e);
    }

public class DirectoryNode extends Component {

    // These constants identify the current node state.

    public static final int HIGH_LIGHTED = 1;
    public static final int SELECTED = 2;
    public static final int RELEASED = 3;
```

```
// These constants identify the node type.

    public static final String DIR = "Dir";
    public static final String FILE = "File";
    public static final String ROOT = "Root";

    protected int nodeState;    // State of node firing
                                // event
    protected String nodeName;  // Name of file or
                                // directory
    protected String nodeType;  // Three types: "File",
                                // "Dir", and "Root".

    protected Vector listeners; // Used to register
                                // listeners
    DirectoryNodeEvent event;

    public DirectoryNode (String nodeType, String
                                nodeName) {

    nodeState = RELEASED;       // Default state
    listeners = new Vector ();  // Used to store
                                // listeners
    this.nodeType = nodeType;
    this.nodeName = nodeName;
    setNodeColors ();
    setUpMouse ();
    repaint ();                 // Parent method
}

/* The user determines the node state by the foreground
   and background colors.*/
protected void setNodeColors () {
  switch (nodeState) {
    case 1:  // HIGH_LIGHTED
      setBackground (Color.magenta);
      setForeground (Color.cyan.brighter());
      break;
    case 2:  // SELECTED
      setBackground (Color.black);
```

```
        setForeground (Color.yellow.brighter());
        break;
      case 3:  // RELEASED
        setBackground (Color.blue);
        setForeground (Color.cyan.brighter());
    }
  }
/* This method sets up code to handle mouse clicks by
  registering an anonymous local class as the mouse
  listener for this component.*/
  protected void setUpMouse () {
    addMouseListener (new MouseAdapter () {
      public void mousePressed (MouseEvent e) {
        switch (nodeState) {
        case 1:  // HIGH_LIGHTED
        nodeState = SELECTED; break;
        case 2:  //SELECTED
        nodeState = RELEASED; break;
        case 3:  // RELEASED
        nodeState = HIGH_LIGHTED;
        }
        setNodeColors (); // Node colors are changed.
        repaint ();// Parent method

  /* The following three statements construct a node event,
    and notify listeners of the state change. */
    DirectoryNode dirNode = DirectoryNode.this;
    event = new DirectoryNodeEvent (dirNode,
        nodeType, nodeName, nodeState);
    notifyListeners (event);
    }
  });
  }


/* The paint() method draws the rectangle representing
  the node, labels the node with: (1) its type ("Root",
  "Dir", or "File"), and (2) its name (file name or
  directory name).*/
  public void paint (Graphics g) {
    Dimension size = getSize ();   // Parent sets size
```

```
     g.setColor (getForeground ()); // Get foreground
                                    // color
     g.drawRect (0, 0, size.width-1, size.height-1);
     g.drawString (nodeType + " " + nodeName,
         size.width/5, size.height/2);
   }
   public Dimension getPreferredSize () {
     return new Dimension (20, 60);
   }
   public Dimension getMinimumSize () {
     return new Dimension (15, 45);
   }

/* The next two methods add and remove listeners from a
   Vector of listener objects (see field declarations,above).
   The Vector class of java.util can be instantiated as an
   expansible array of objects. */
   public void addDirectoryNodeListener
         (DirectoryNodeListener l) {
     if (!listeners.contains (l)) listeners.addElement (l);
   }
   public void removeDirectoryNodeListener
         (DirectoryNodeListener l) {
     listeners.removeElement (l);
   }

/* This method is synchronized so the listeners will not
   change until this event has been processed. The Vector
   is converted to an Enumeration so the array of
   listeners can be traversed by the while loop. */
   protected synchronized void notifyListeners
         (DirectoryNodeEvent event) {
     Enumeration e = listeners.elements ();
     while (e.hasMoreElements ()) {
       DirectoryNodeListener l =
         (DirectoryNodeListener) e.nextElement ();
       l.nodeStateChanged (event);
     }
   }
}
```

```
class DirectoryNodeTest extends Applet
        implements DirectoryNodeListener {

  TextField textfield;
  DirectoryNode node;

  public void init () {

    node = new DirectoryNode ("Dir", "Current_dir");
    node.addDirectoryNodeListener (this);
    textfield = new TextField ("default state = RELEASED");
    setLayout (new BorderLayout ());
    add (textfield, BorderLayout.NORTH);
    add (node, BorderLayout.CENTER);
  }
  public void nodeStateChanged (DirectoryNodeEvent e) {

    switch (e.getNodeState ()) {
      case 1:  // HIGH_LIGHTED
      textfield.setText ("node state = HIGH_LIGHTED");
      break;
      case 2:  // SELECTED
      textfield.setText ("node state = SELECTED");
      break;
      case 3:  // RELEASED:
      textfield.setText ("node state = RELEASED");
    }
  }
}
```

8.2 Java Beans

A Java bean is a reusable software component that can be visually manipulated by a "beanbox" tool. One such tool is provided as part of JavaSoft's Bean Development Kit (BDK). The BDK includes the JavaBeans Application Programming Interface (API) (see Figure 8.4). The BDK is not part of the Java Development Kit (JDK), and usually must be downloaded or obtained separately.

8.2.1 Levels of Bean Programmers

There are three levels of bean programmers:

1. Beanbox tool programmers who write code for application builders, GUI editors, etc.

2. Bean authors

3. Programmers of applications who use beans or combinations of beans (usually with the aid of beanbox tools)

8.2.2 Bean Properties

An application programmer customizes a bean by setting the values of its properties, as shown in Figure 8.2. A bean property is a piece of its internal state (usually represented by an instance variable) that can be set and queried.

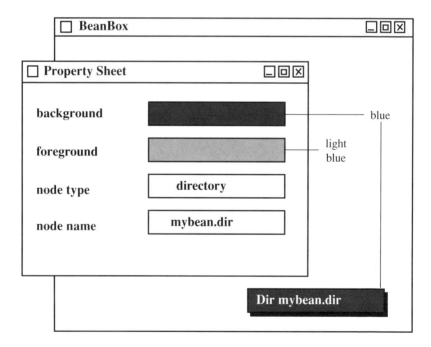

Figure 8.2 Editing Bean Properties with BeanBox Tools

Bean properties are usually set during the "design phase." This is done directly, when a beanbox tool sets and queries bean properties, or indirectly, when the beanbox relies on the classes and methods of the JavaBeans API for access. Whether the access is direct or indirect, bean classes must provide accessor methods. This is because fields that represent bean properties are not allowed to be declared public. According to the JavaBeans standard, accessor methods must follow a strict naming convention. For example, the `java.awt.Component` class includes the `setValid()` and `setVisible()` methods which have valid accessor names (the criteria for which will be discussed). Thus, the Component class is a valid bean, although it is seldom used as such.

8.2.3 JavaBeans Application Programming Interface (API)

A bean *exports* to the JavaBeans API its events, properties, and also any public non-accessor methods. During runtime, the primary means of communication between beans is the *firing* of events. Also, events provide a way to connect beans during "design time" (see Figure 8.3). A bean's properties are used mostly during design for the purpose of customization. Non-accessor public methods are rarely used.

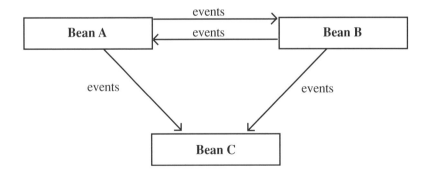

Figure 8.3 Beans Connected by Events

It is permissible to write invisible beans, but at the same time, they may be visually manipulated by the beanbox tool.

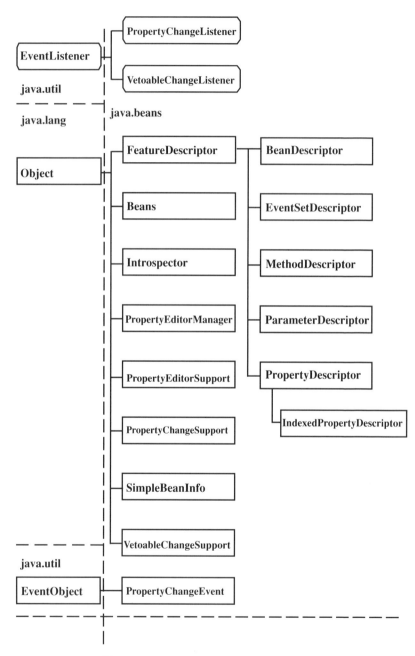

Figure 8.4 The `java.beans` Package

The java.beans package (see Figure 8.4) is used by programmers of beanbox tools and by bean authors. Programmers of applications who use beans do not need to know about the classes and interfaces contained in java.beans.

The bean author can have additional information to be displayed by implementing the BeanInfo interface. One way this can be done is by subclassing SimpleBeanInfo, which is a simplified implementation of BeanInfo. The naming convention that will cause a beanbox tool to instantiate the appropiate BeanInfo object is: the name of the bean with BeanInfo appended (e.g., MyBeanBeanInfo). The BeanInfo implementation may, in turn, specify feature descriptor objects. For example, text explaining a bean's properties would be included in a PropertyDescriptor object.

The property sheet of beanbox tools is sufficient for editing most properties. For more complex properties, such as enumerations or graphic displays, the bean author may create a property editor by implementing the PropertyEditor interface. The editor for a specific property can be registered with the beanbox tool by invoking the registerEditor() method of the PropertyEditorManager class, the setPropertyEditor() method of the PropertyDescriptor class, or simply by following the naming convention of appending Editor to the property name (e.g., MyPropertyEditor would be automatically registered as the editor of myProperty).

The java.bean.Beans class does not have to be extended to create a valid bean; however, it has two important methods: instantiate() and isInstanceOf(). Bean programmers should not use the new or instanceof operators, but should rely on the Beans.instantiate() and Beans.isInstanceOf() methods.

8.2.4 Bean Design Phase

Bean properties allow a programmer to customize a bean at design time. Also, although the primary means of communication between beans is events, other beans, and code in general, can interact with a bean by invoking its property accessor methods.

Unlike most software library modules, beans are instantiated and become alive during the design phase of an application. If a new property value is typed into a bean's property sheet (see Figure 8.2), there is usually an immediate change (e.g., its background color changes). Also, if a designer were to connect an invisible clock bean to a visible bean, the visible bean might be programmed to pulsate (periodically expand and contract as the color lightens and darkens) in response to the event "fired" by the clock bean (see Figure 8.2).

8.2.5 Accessing Bean Properties

Instance variables that hold property values usually are declared with the protected access modifier. Accessor methods made available to get and set properties must be declared public. If a property is stored in an instance field named `propertyName` whose type is `propertyType`, the getter method's prototype takes the following form:

public propertyType getPropertyName ();

The setter method for the same property would take this form:

public void setPropertyName (propertyType parameter);

For boolean properties, there is a special accessor method whose prototype takes this form:

public boolean isBooleanName ();

It is important to remember that the first letter of the property name is not capitalized, but the first letter following the get, set, or is must be. The following are examples of bean properties and their corresponding accessor methods:

```
protected int height, width;
protected Color foregroundColor;
protected FontMetrics fontMetrics;
protected boolean greater;
public int getHeight () { return height };
public void setWidth (int newWidth) { width = newWidth };
public FontMetrics getFontMetrics () {return fontMetrics};
public void setForegroundColor (Color fgc)
    { foregroundColor = fgc };
public boolean isGreater () { return greater };
```

8.2.6 Bound Properties

A bound property is one which causes an event to be fired if its value is changed. The prototypes for the PropertyChangeEvent class (see Figure 8.4) are shown below:

```
public class PropertyChangeEvent extends EventObject {
// Public Constructor
  public PropertyChangeEvent (Object source,
                              String propertyName,
                              Object oldValue,
                              Object newValue);
// Public Methods
  public Object getOldValue ();
  public Object getNewValue ();
  public Object getPropagationId ();
  public String getName ();
  public void setPropagationId (Object propagationId);
}
```

The PropertyChangeSupport class and the PropertyEditorSupport classes both include the addPropertyChangeListener() and removePropertyChangeListener() methods.

8.2.7 Converting a Custom GUI Component to a Bean

Any custom GUI component can be converted to a bean without too much difficulty. The first task involves the custom component's constructors. Although it is not a formal bean requirement, most beanbox tools expect a no-argument constructor. Therefore, the programmer should either verify, or create, such a constructor. Next the programmer must determine which fields of the custom component will be used to represent bean properties. Any field that will represent a property should be declared protected, and that field must be accessible by valid getter and setter methods.

A good example of a prospective bean is the custom GUI component represented by the DirectoryNode class (shown in Figure 8.1). The DirectoryNode class does not have a no-argument constructor, which means one must be created. The simplest way to do this is to write a no-argument constructor that invokes one of the existing constructors, and that passes it default values as parameters (see no-argument constructor, below). Once this aspect has been dealt with, the next step is to determine which DirectoryNode fields will be used to represent bean properties. The two most obvious prospects are nodeName and nodeType, because it would be useful to set the name and type of a node during the design phase of an application. Conveniently, nodeName and nodeType are already declared protected, but there are no associated getter or setter methods. Thus, to allow access, getter and setter methods for nodeName and nodeType must be created (see accessor methods below).

```
public class DirectoryNode extends Component {
// Constants for the new DirectoryNode bean will go here

// These fields are bean properties

    protected String nodeName; // Name of file or directory
    protected String nodeType; // Three types: "File",
                               // "Dir", and "Root".

// Other bean instance fields will go here
// Beanbox tool will call no-argument constructor

public DirectoryNode () {

this ("node type", "node name"); // Default values
}

public DirectoryNode (String nodeType, String nodeName) {

  nodeState = RELEASED;      // Default state
  listeners = new Vector (); // Used to store listeners
  this.nodeType = nodeType;
  this.nodeName = nodeName;
  setNodeColors ();
  setUpMouse ();
  repaint ();
}
```

```
/* The user determines the node state by the foreground
   and background colors. */
   protected void setNodeColors () {
// Body of setNodeColors
}
    ...
// Accessor methods for bean properties

   public String getNodeType () { return nodeType };
   public String getNodeName () { return nodeName };
   public void setNodeType (String nodeType)
      { this.nodeType = nodeType };
   public void setNodeName (String nodeName)
   { this.nodeName = nodeName };
}
```

Making the above changes would result in a valid, workable bean, but only limited customization of DirectoryNode would be possible. This is because the bean would only have two programmable properties: nodeName and nodeType. Its flexibility could be enhanced by allowing the application programmer to set the foreground and background colors for each of the three states: HIGH_LIGHTED, SELECTED, and RELEASED.

8.2.8 Specification of Bean Information

The Introspector class (see Figure 8.4) is never instantiated. However, application builders utilize its static getBeanInfo() method to obtain bean information. For a bean class named xxx, getBeanInfo() first looks for a xxxBeanInfo class. If none is found, it relies upon the introspection mechanism found in the java.lang.reflect package to obtain information about the bean's properties, events, and exported methods.

8.3   Java Swing Components

The Abstract Windowing Toolkit (AWT) provides the components that can be combined to form GUIs. The AWT components are referred to as "heavyweight" components because they rely on already existing "peer" components found on specific platforms. For example, the Mac platform button component was designed in the Motif style, so its appearance differs somewhat from its UNIX or Windows counterpart.

Java Swing components are called "lightweight" components because they are independent of existing peers. Lightweight components have the advantage that they appear (and behave) exactly the same on different systems, and also, applications that rely on these components are more likely to be bug free.

There are three important concepts about Swing components:

1. For every `java.awt` component there is a `java.awt.swing` counterpart, and the class name of the counterpart components always begin with "J" (e.g., `JFrame`, `JButton`, `JMenu`, etc.).

2. Swing components generally have more functionality than AWT components.

3. The `java.awt.swing` package includes additional components for which there is no `java.awt` counterpart.

In the next several sections, we will describe some of the ways Swing components are improvements of their AWT counterparts and also some additional components for which there is no `java.awt` counterpart.

8.3.1 JFrame – Improved from AWT Frame Counterpart

The `JFrame` component differs from the AWT frame in that it has an additional layer of containment, the `ContentPane`. Components should always be added to a `JFrame` by using the `getContentPane()` method, for example:

```
getContentPane.add (textarea, BorderLayout.NORTH);
```

8.3.2 JTabbedPane – New Component Type

The onscreen appearance of a `JTabbedPane` is similar to the tabs of files in a drawer. The individual tabs are added to a `TabbedPane` by `addTab()`, an overloaded method with different parameter lists. The `addTab()` version with the greatest functionality is shown below:

public void addTab (*String* label, Icon icon,
                     Component component, *String* tooltip);

The first parameter, label, refers to the string that identifies the tab (see Figure 8.4); icon is a reference to an object used to draw an icon next to the label; component identifies a component that will appear if the tab is selected; and tooltip refers to a string that will appear if the mouse cursor is passed over the tab. There are also versions of the addTab() method without a tooltip parameter and with neither a tooltip nor an icon parameter.

The tabs are added in a row until it runs out of room, then a new row is added. The JTabbedPane is added to the JFrame by the following statement:

getContentPane.add (JTabbedPane, BorderLayout.SOUTH);

An instance of a class that implements the Icon interface is supplied as the addTab() method's second argument, if an icon is desired. This interface has three methods:

public int getIconWidth ();
public int getIconHeight ();
public void paintIcon (Component component, Graphics g,
                    int x, *int* y);

8.3.3 JButton – Improved from AWT Button Counterpart

The JButton component allows the programmer to specify three different icons (depending on the status of the button), the position of the text relative to the icon, and the style of the buttons border.

```
JButton button;
// The button is created with the default icon.
  button = new JButton ("Start", new BtnIcon (Color.cyan, 4));
  button.setVerticalTextPosition (JButton.TOP);
  button.setPressedIcon (new BtnIcon (Color.red, 3));
  button.setRolloverIcon (new BtnIcon (Color.blue, 2));
  button.setBorder (BorderFactory.createBevelBorder ());
```

The PressedIcon is the icon that will be displayed after the button has been pressed. The RollOverIcon is the icon that will be displayed when the mouse cursor passes over it. The code for the BtnIcon class is presented below:

```
class BtnIcon implements Icon {
  private int bw;
  private Color color;
  BtnIcon (Color color, int borderWidth) {
    this.color = color;
    bw = borderWidth;
  }
  public void paintIcon (Component c, Graphics g, int x, int y)
  { g.setColor (Color.blue);
    g.fillRect (x, y, getIconWidth(), getIconHeight());
    g.setColor (color);
    g.fillRect (x + bw, y + bw, getIconWidth() - bw * 2,
      getIconHeight() - bw * 2);
  }
  public int getIconWidth () { return 15; }
  public int getIconHeight () { return 15; }
}
```

8.3.4 New Swing Components – Toggle Buttons, Radio Buttons, Combo Boxes, and Toolbars

JToggleButton

A toggle button is similar to a check box. It only has two states, selected and unselected, but it is different in that it indicates its state by altering the appearance of the button rather than by a checkmark. The JToggleButton class has seven constructors that allow the toggle button to be created with a label, or an icon, or both a label and an icon, or neither (a constructor with no arguments). Also, its initial state may be optionally specified by a boolean parameter. The constructor with the most functionality is shown below:

```
public JToggleButton (String label, Icon icon, boolean
                selected_state);
```

JRadioButton

Swing radio buttons offer almost the same functionality as the type of AWT check boxes that are part of a check box group. However, because both the look and functionality of radio buttons is different from the look and functionality of check boxes, it is more convenient to have a radio button class that is separate from the class used to create check boxes (the AWT uses Checkbox for both). The following code exemplifies the use of JRadioButton:

```
JRadioButton firstRadio = new JRadioButton ("1st Choice", 1);
JRadioButton secondRadio = new JRadioButton
          ("2nd Choice", 2);
ButtonGroup buttonGroup = new ButtonGroup ();
buttonGroup.add (firstRadio);
add (firstRadio);    // Add to current container
buttonGroup.add (secondRadio);
add (secondRadio);   // Add to current container
```

JComboBox

The Swing combo box is similar in functionality to that of the AWT choice component. The combo box does, however, have an important improvement: it allows the programmer to specify the maximum number of displayed choices. If the number of choices exceeds the maximum, the combo box includes a scrollbar, so the user can examine the choices not initially displayed. The following code will create a combo box and add it to the current container:

```
static final String fishes = { bass, trout, salmon, catfish,
                               sturgeon, halibut };

    . . .
JComboBox comboBox = new JComboBox (fishes);
comboBox.setMaximumRowCount (4);      // Four items
                                      // displayed
comboBox.setSelectedItem ("salmon");  // Initial selection
add (comboBox);                       // Add to current
                                      // container
```

JToolBar

A toolbar is an elongated, rectangular window that contains other components. Aside from its shape, the most important characteristic of a toolbar is that the user may detach it and place it in another window. The following code will create a toolbar and add it to the current container:

```
JToolBar toolBar = new JToolBar ();
setLayout (new BorderLayout ());
// Code to create radio buttons
toolBar.add (firstRadio);
toolBar.add (secondRadio);
add (toolBar, BorderLayout.NORTH);
```

REA's Test Preps
The Best in Test Preparation

- REA "Test Preps" are **far more** comprehensive than any other test preparation series
- Each book contains up to **eight** full-length practice tests based on the most recent exams
- **Every** type of question likely to be given on the exams is included
- Answers are accompanied by **full** and **detailed** explanations

REA has published over 60 Test Preparation volumes in several series. They include:

Advanced Placement Exams (APs)
Biology
Calculus AB & Calculus BC
Chemistry
Computer Science
English Language & Composition
English Literature & Composition
European History
Government & Politics
Physics
Psychology
Statistics
Spanish Language
United States History

College-Level Examination Program (CLEP)
Analyzing and Interpreting Literature
College Algebra
Freshman College Composition
General Examinations
General Examinations Review
History of the United States I
Human Growth and Development
Introductory Sociology
Principles of Marketing
Spanish

SAT II: Subject Tests
American History
Biology E/M
Chemistry
English Language Proficiency Test
French
German

SAT II: Subject Tests (cont'd)
Literature
Mathematics Level IC, IIC
Physics
Spanish
Writing

Graduate Record Exams (GREs)
Biology
Chemistry
Computer Science
Economics
Engineering
General
History
Literature in English
Mathematics
Physics
Psychology
Sociology

ACT - ACT Assessment

ASVAB - Armed Services Vocational Aptitude Battery

CBEST - California Basic Educational Skills Test

CDL - Commercial Driver License Exam

CLAST - College-Level Academic Skills Test

ELM - Entry Level Mathematics

ExCET - Exam for the Certification of Educators in Texas

FE (EIT) - Fundamentals of Engineering Exam

FE Review - Fundamentals of Engineering Review

GED - High School Equivalency Diploma Exam (U.S. & Canadian editions)

GMAT - Graduate Management Admission Test

LSAT - Law School Admission Test

MAT - Miller Analogies Test

MCAT - Medical College Admission Test

MSAT - Multiple Subjects Assessment for Teachers

NJ HSPT- New Jersey High School Proficiency Test

PPST - Pre-Professional Skills Tests

PRAXIS II/NTE - Core Battery

PSAT - Preliminary Scholastic Assessment Test

SAT I - Reasoning Test

SAT I - Quick Study & Review

TASP - Texas Academic Skills Program

TOEFL - Test of English as a Foreign Language

TOEIC - Test of English for International Communication

RESEARCH & EDUCATION ASSOCIATION
61 Ethel Road W. • Piscataway, New Jersey 08854
Phone: (732) 819-8880   **website: www.rea.com**

Please send me more information about your Test Prep books

Name _____

Address _____

City _____ State _____ Zip _____